LOVE FOOD

FAMILY

RECIPES FROM the KITCHEN DISCO

SOPHIE ELLIS-BEXTOR *and* RICHARD JONES

hamlyn

contents

FOOD-LOVING FAMILY

Ooh, isn't this exciting? A cookbook! A dream come true for us, given that we have spent much of our nearly two decades together getting excited about the food we are about to eat, making ourselves things to eat, or reminiscing about delicious things we've eaten together or on the road… and then trying to make them at home. In fact, all the big events that have happened in our relationship – babies, albums, celebrations or quieter moments – all of them have had a soundtrack and a taste. Probably a cocktail or two, as well. Food is always there, along for the ride with music on in the background, while we enjoy whatever we've just put on the table.

And there's no stopping that train any time soon. We now find ourselves the only two grown-ups at the head of a big family: two adults and five kids, to be precise. Both mama and papa in the house also happen to be musicians, and our two big, enduring loves in life are music and food.

We can spend many happy hours listening to music we love while we eat food we love, or talk about what we get to eat next… In fact, we are the sort of people who go to bed excited about the fact we get to have breakfast when we get up. It's that kind of household.

Luckily, not only do we love food but we love making ourselves things to eat, and we very much hope our little boys also develop a love of the simple but infinite joy that comes from making yourself something tasty. It's a science that never gets dull and a friend for life. Plus, we want them all to cook for us one day.

So, this book? Well, it's a love letter to the things we like to eat and recipes we enjoy making. It contains all our favourites and the dishes the kids like to eat. But not just us: the grandparents, Grandma Janet and Grandad Tony, they're here; Auntie Martha is here; Uncle Jackson is here and others are too, all are in these pages, as that's how it goes with food in our house. Let's cook! Let's cook together! Then let's eat like kings!

When you flick through the pages you're going to find food for kids, food for quick and healthy midweek suppers, communal food for friends, food from our travels around the world, Sunday lunches, food for special occasions, and much more. We've also put in our tips for making meals that suit the various needs of a large table. If you want your dinner with more spice than your neighbour, we can help with that, too.

For the most part, we like to cook quick stuff that's delicious and healthy. We're fairly impatient so we don't want to spend hours on it. Maybe once in a blue moon that's fun, and it's a nice way to spoil ourselves, but mostly we just want to make something that goes from fridge to plate in 30 minutes or so. Sometimes there's a bit of slow cooking involved, but the prep never takes long. That being said, we still want our food to be full of flavour and to make a good-looking, colourful meal. We don't want to waste our hunger on something that doesn't hit the spot.

We both think making yourself something that is nutritious but also delicious is a way to be kind to yourself as well as one of life's big pleasures. This has been the case since we were young. Teenage Sophie would head home in school lunchbreak to make herself something to eat and grew up helping out in the kitchen. Richard grew up the son of a chef, so cooking is in his genes. From his early childhood, his dad

Tony would talk to him about the time he did his training and worked in the kitchen at the famous Café Royal in London in the swinging Sixties. He has amazing stories from that time – like serving 'baked Vesuvius' to the Beatles at an album launch, cooking for the Kray twins who popped in on a regular basis to have their supper, while Tom Jones was frequently found hanging out at the bar. Being around music and food is at least two generations old for the Jones men.

It's been pretty integral to our life together that we both love to cook as, though neither of us are chefs in any sense, our love of food has always been such a key part of our story. Not just in the literal sense, but also in the way music and food are intertwined both on and off stage. Obviously, our music has introduced us to new culinary experiences when we tour, but also we've noticed that the way a dish is created isn't dissimilar to the layers in a song. You have your bass notes and rhythm (mashed potato, chips, rice, pasta), then the guitars and keys in the middle (steak, sausage, fish, aubergines), then the top layer comes with the notes of the vocals and percussion (salt, pepper, herbs and spice). It's all a balance, a mix, that comes together in endless variations but with the same principles throughout. When you get it just right, then just like a brilliantly produced piece of music, it all comes together in your mouth… it's a hit!

We can be quite competitive about food sometimes. When one of us is on tour, it is not unheard of for the other one at home to take a photo of whatever supper they've made and send it to the one who's away – just to make them jealous. That being said, nothing is as lovely as cooking a meal for loved ones. We actually wooed each other with food: a homemade lobster casserole was our first Valentine's meal, and it was delicious.

Along the way, our cooking has evolved and with all our small people, we now have a constant café in the kitchen. One thing is for sure in a big household – there's always someone (or something, we have cats too) that wants to be fed. There are also lots of times in which we'll have friends over, or maybe the kids have a couple of mates over, or maybe it's a nice day so, hey, why not have a BBQ? Basically, all roads lead to food, to many mouths to feed, so no one leaves our home hungry. Not on our watch.

That doesn't mean it's always plain sailing. Cooking for seven people thrice daily means seven different sets of tastebuds. We have a vegetarian: ten-year-old Ray who made his decision without drama and was tested early on when it was beef burgers for supper one night. He has stayed the distance and it suits him. We also have 'eats-pretty-much-everything' six-year-old Jesse; thirteen-year-old Kit who is very exacting with good instincts, but would rather go hungry than eat stuff he doesn't like; Sonny, now eighteen, who is happy to eat but doesn't dance around with joy at the prospect of 'what to eat next', he knows what he likes and pretty much sticks to that; and then we have three-year-old Mickey who likes a lot but, you know, is not keen on spice. All of these preferences are subject to change, as is typical with small folk, so by the time this is in print… it's probably all changed.

But we should be honest with you: we cannot say that everything we serve is eaten to a clean plate by all at the table. As anyone with many mouths to feed would probably agree, a successful meal is one where the *majority* of mouths eat the *majority* of the meal. However we have learnt as we go and the recipes you find here – the family favourites – are just that. From top to bottom of our family tree, we have now got these recipes just how we like them and we're so happy to share them with you.

Whatever we're up to, the How, Where and What of all we will eat is a conversation we are having all the time, whether it's what the kids are having for supper, what we're having communally at the weekend, what to cook for friends when they come over... even what to cook in the studio sometimes (we cooked for the band and engineers when we made Sophie's last two records). Cooking to us is a way to extend nurture, thoughtfulness and gratitude to those around us. Affection on a plate, basically. When folk come over for supper or Sunday lunch, we don't want them to witness a stressful situation where we're bending over backwards to create tricky culinary masterpieces. We're not trying to impress here, we just want them to enter a place where the prep is done, the wine is open, the oven is on and the music is playing. Eating together should be happy, chilled and comforting. It's not about showing off, but about showing love. We were both raised that way.

Talking of being raised one way or another, we have two promises we made to ourselves when it comes to the kids: they will leave home being able to cook and to dance. Maybe at the same time... Well, it's no coincidence that our kitchen is also the place where we have our sound system, our turntable, our flashing lights and our disco ball. This ended up all making some kind of crazy sense when, at the start of the UK's lockdown in March 2020, we found ourselves broadcasting discos live from our home. Singing into the camera on the back of Richard's phone, Sophie would put on sequins and sing songs while trying not to trip over the kids. They were home concerts at a time where we couldn't go out so, of course, they were kitchen discos. We didn't invent them, but we did live them – the lockdown days were a mix of domesticity and discos and not much else for the many months that followed.

But back to the here and now and the roads that have brought us to making this book. It's important to us that you know this is a book not from the point of view of two chefs, but two people who adore making things to eat and want to give folk the confidence to think they can do it too. We believe that anyone and everyone can cook. Like the mighty Nigel Slater says, if you can make yourself a cup of tea, you can cook. It's just ingredients and timing when you think about it. So if you've never cooked before, welcome! We hope you find things that give you courage in the kitchen. We've also chucked in the stories that go with the food as that's how it goes, right? How can you eat something and love it without all the memories flooding back as the taste hits? Isn't it so clever what's hidden in the mouthfuls?

Above all, we hope you have fun. We hope these pages end up sticky from the times you've made the recipes that lie within. Let's put on the playlists, pour the cocktails and get stuck in… it's all done with lots of love from our house to yours – a real-life family with their real-life cooking. A family who blooming love food.

Sophie and Richard

THE PLAYLISTS

If music be the love of food, let's make a playlist! That's definitely the case round here… In our home there's always a tune playing on the stereo while we make ourselves something to eat. Well, what did you expect from a singer and a bassist who love to cook? And, of course, all our kids have their favourite songs to dance to, so that's part of the set, too.

We believe that hearing the right songs can put you in the right mood, which in turn will help you get that meal on the table. With this in mind, we've curated playlists for every chapter in the book, and they have been really fun to put together. We'll update them if we find new songs we think work, too, so it's an ever-evolving sonic landscape from our kitchen to yours.

Within these playlists you'll find a musical companion just for you, whether you're enjoying a Sunday roast or a big party feast. No matter what page you flip to, there's a song to bring the atmosphere. Whatever the occasion, we've got you covered. There have been so many times when we've heard a song and it's reminded us of something good we ate, or maybe a delicious drink we had, and we hope these tunes do the same for you. Maybe our favourite bit is saved for, you guessed it, the cocktail chapter. Waiting for you there is our ultimate kitchen disco playlist. It's a Friday night for the soul, no matter what the clock or the calendar say.

We hope you enjoy all the tracks we've put together. And we hope they give your ears a treat as you relish your time in the kitchen. I mean, there's no need to make a song and dance about it, but it helps!

To access the playlist, scan the QR code on your smartphone or go to www.sophieellisbextor.net/kitchendiscoplaylists

Enjoy!

GOOD
OLD
BLIGHTY♥

It's the place we call home and actually, home to a lot of the food we adore! Stews, roasts, Yorkshire puds and pies... within this chapter lie the greatest hits of British food (except for the saintly fish and chips, which we leave to the chip shops of the land. Oh, with a gherkin too, please, and as much vinegar, ketchup and mayonnaise as my heart desires).

ROAST DINNER – RIB OF BEEF & PERFECT GRAVY

IF WE WANT A ROAST DINNER THAT FEEDS THE MASSES AND LOOKS INCREDIBLE ON THE TABLE, THEN ROAST BEEF IT IS. CARAMELISED AND BROWN OUTSIDE, PINK AND SUCCULENT WITHIN, IT MELTS IN THE MOUTH AND HITS THE SPOT LIKE NO OTHER ROAST. PLUS THE LEFTOVERS ARE GOOD, TOO!

1 large rib of beef (2.5–3kg/5lb 8oz–6lb 8oz), remove from the fridge at least an hour before cooking to allow it to come to room temperature
3 onions, chopped into 6 wedges
2 carrots, chopped into 3cm (1¼ inch) pieces
4 celery sticks, chopped into 3cm (1¼ inch) pieces
6 garlic cloves (in their skins)
1 bunch of thyme
4 rosemary sprigs
3 tablespoons olive oil
salt and black pepper

FOR THE GRAVY
1 tablespoon plain flour
150ml (5fl oz) red wine
750ml (generous 1¼ pints) good-quality beef stock
1 tablespoon Dijon mustard
salt and black pepper

Preheat the oven to 220°C (475°F), Gas Mark 9. Calculate your required roasting time: 15 minutes per 500g/1lb 2oz for rare; 17 minutes per 500g/1lb 2oz for medium-rare; 20 minutes per 500g/1lb 2oz for medium; plus 30 minutes resting time.

In a large roasting tray, toss the vegetables, garlic cloves and herbs in 2 tablespoons of the olive oil and a good pinch of salt.

Pat the surface of the beef dry with kitchen paper. Using your hands, coat the beef with the remaining tablespoon of olive oil and season with salt and pepper. Place the beef on top of the vegetables in the tray.

Roast for 20 minutes, then turn the oven temperature down to 170°C (375°F), Gas Mark 5 and cook for the remaining time calculated. You can use a temperature probe to check that the meat is cooked according to your preference: 50°C (122°F) for rare; 54°C (129°F) for medium-rare; 58°C (136°F) for medium.

Lift the meat out of the tray, loosely wrap in foil and allow to rest for 30 minutes while you get on with the gravy.

Place the roasting tray over a medium-high heat. Sprinkle over the flour and stir well, scraping any bits from the bottom. Allow the flour to cook out for 3–4 minutes, stirring continuously, until it has browned slightly. Pour in the wine, stirring vigorously, then pour in the beef stock. Bring to the boil, then reduce the heat and simmer for 15 minutes, again stirring regularly. Carefully sieve the gravy and return it to the heat, then stir through the mustard and taste for seasoning.

Carve up the beef and serve alongside the gravy and any sides you like. We recommend Nanny Claire's Yorkshire Pudding, Roast Potatoes and Lemony Cavolo Nero (see pages 16–17).

nanny claire's Yorkshire pudding

NANNY CLAIRE WAS OUR KIDS' NANNY FOR OVER 10 YEARS, SO SHE'S FAMILY. THIS HUGE TRAY-BAKED YORKSHIRE PUD IS ONE OF HER SIGNATURE DISHES AND ALSO ONE OF OUR FAVOURITE KINDS OF CHEMISTRY. BATTER IN, 20 MINUTES LATER A GOLDEN, GINORMOUS TRAY OF GOODNESS. WE EAT ONE WITH EVERY ROAST WE MAKE.

SERVES 6

140g (5oz) plain flour
4 free-range eggs
200ml (7fl oz) milk
light olive oil
a little black pepper

Preheat the oven to 220°C (475°F), Gas Mark 9.

Put all the ingredients, apart from the oil, into a large mixing bowl and whisk until you have a smooth batter. Leave to rest for 30 minutes.

Pour in enough oil to cover ½ cm (¼ inch) of the base of a 30 × 25cm (12 × 10 inch) tin and put into the oven for 10 minutes so it gets really hot.

Carefully remove the tray from the oven and pour in the batter. Return to the oven to cook for 20–25 minutes until puffed up and golden. My rule is: don't open the door when it's cooking! If you do, the pudding can collapse – it needs the heat for the magic to happen. Sometimes, it cooks a little quicker, so you can peek in on it after about 18 minutes.

Season with black pepper and serve with roast beef and gravy (see page 14).

ROAST POTATOES

SERVES 6

2kg (4lb 8oz) potatoes (Maris Piper or russets),
  peeled and cut into 5cm (2 inch) chunks
4 tablespoons olive oil/goose fat/vegetable oil
  (whatever your preference is), plus extra
  for drizzling
2 tablespoons semolina (optional)
1 garlic bulb, split into cloves
3 rosemary sprigs
splash of malt vinegar
salt and black pepper

Preheat the oven to 200°C (425°F), Gas Mark 7.

Place the prepped potatoes into a large pan of cold
water as you go so that they don't discolour. Season
the water generously with salt, then set the pan over
a medium-high heat and bring to the boil. Reduce to
a simmer and cook for 15 minutes until fork tender.

Meanwhile, pour your chosen oil or fat into your
largest roasting tray and put it in the oven to get
nice and hot.

When the potatoes are tender, drain in a colander,
then leave to steam for a few minutes. Return to the
pan and shake a few times to fluff up the potatoes.
As an added extra for more crunch, you can
sprinkle over the semolina and shake again.

Remove the tray from the oven, carefully tip the
potatoes into the hot oil and lightly toss. Roast for
35 minutes, then remove from the oven.

Using the flat edge of a chef's knife, firmly smash
the garlic cloves along with the rosemary and mix
in a small bowl with some malt vinegar, a little
olive oil and some salt and pepper and add these to
the tray. Toss, then return the tray to the oven for a
further 20–25 minutes until the potatoes are deeply
golden and crisp.

LEMONY CAVOLO NERO

SERVES 6

400g (14oz) cavolo nero
3 tablespoons olive oil
juice of 1 lemon
salt and black pepper

If the cavolo nero stems are particularly thick and
fibrous (especially towards the bottom), remove the
leaves from the stems. Slice the leaves into 3cm
(1¼ inch) pieces.

Heat half of the olive oil in your largest frying pan
over a high heat. When the oil is shimmering, add
half of the cavolo nero and fry for 2–3 minutes.
Leave undisturbed as much as possible so that it
has a chance to develop some colour, stirring only
as necessary to ensure it fries evenly. Transfer to a
bowl and repeat with the remaining oil and cavolo
nero. When the second batch is cooked, return
the first batch to the pan, add the lemon juice and
season to taste with salt and pepper.

Pictured overleaf ☞

GRANDMA JANET'S ROAST SPATCHCOCK CHICKEN
WITH BREAD SAUCE

SERVES 4

1.25kg (2lb 12oz) whole chicken (ask the butcher to spatchcock it)
1 garlic bulb, halved widthways
1 lemon, thinly sliced
2 rosemary sprigs, broken up
2 tablespoons olive oil
salt and black pepper

FOR THE BREAD SAUCE
1 onion, peeled
8 cloves
2 bay leaves
6 black peppercorns
600ml (20fl oz) full-fat milk, or as needed
½ loaf of stale good-quality white bread (about 250g/9oz), crusts removed
40g (1½oz) salted butter
salt and black pepper

FOR THE SPEEDY GRAVY
300ml (10fl oz) white wine
300ml (10fl oz) chicken stock
1 tablespoon Dijon mustard
salt and black pepper

TO SERVE
store-bought chilli jam or cranberry sauce

IF YOU RANG OUR DOORBELL ON A SUNDAY AFTERNOON, CHANCES ARE THIS IS WHAT WE'D BE EATING. THE COSIEST OF GRANDMA'S HOMECOOKED MEALS, THIS SPATCHCOCK CHICKEN IS A CLEVER WAY TO GET THE ROAST TO YOUR TABLE MUCH QUICKER THAN THE NORMAL METHOD. STAYS JUICY, TOO! PLUS – THE BEST BREAD SAUCE IN THE LAND.

Preheat the oven to 180°C (400°F), Gas Mark 6.

First, infuse the milk for the bread sauce. Stud the onion with cloves. Place in a medium saucepan along with the bay leaves, peppercorns, milk and a pinch of salt. Bring almost to the boil, then remove from the heat, cover and leave to infuse while you prepare the chicken.

Season the chicken well with salt and pepper and place in a snug-fitting roasting tray. Add the garlic, lemon, rosemary and oil and toss everything to coat. Make sure the garlic is cut-side down, then bake for 45–50 minutes, or until the chicken is golden, crisp and the juices run clear when the thickest part of the leg is pierced with a knife.

As the chicken roasts, return to the bread sauce. Roughly tear the bread into chunks, then pulse in a food processor to form coarse breadcrumbs.

Strain the infused milk into a jug, discarding everything left in the sieve, and return to the saucepan over a medium-high heat. Bring to a lively simmer, then gradually stir in nearly all of the breadcrumbs. Bring to a simmer once more, then add the butter, stir well and taste for seasoning. At this point, either add a splash more milk or the remaining breadcrumbs, depending on how thick you like your bread sauce. Adjust the seasoning as needed and keep on a low heat.

Remove the chicken from the tray and leave to rest while you make the speedy gravy. Simply place the tray over a high heat, add the wine, stock and mustard, and give it all a good whisk. Simmer until reduced by half, then taste and adjust the seasoning. Strain through a sieve into a jug.

Carve up the chicken and serve with a really good scoop of bread sauce, a spoonful of chilli jam or cranberry sauce and a drizzle of gravy. If going the whole hog, some greens, Roast Potatoes and Nanny Claire's Yorkshire Pudding (see pages 16 and 17) would also go perfectly here.

COSY BEEF STEW

SERVES 4–6

THE MOST COMFORTING MEAL FOR THE COLDER DAYS THAT COME OUR WAY IN AUTUMN AND WINTER. OUR FAVOURITE BIT ABOUT THIS MEAL IS THE WAY THE STEW THICKENS AND CAN BE SCOOPED UP ON CRUSTY BREAD, THEN WASHED DOWN WITH RED WINE. IT'S LIKE A HUG IN A BOWL.

800g (1lb 12oz) boneless beef shin, trimmed and cut into 5cm (2 inch) chunks
2 tablespoons olive oil, or as needed
2 onions, finely chopped
2 celery sticks, finely chopped
3 garlic cloves, finely sliced
4 bay leaves
5 thyme sprigs
2 tablespoons tomato purée
500ml (18fl oz) red wine
3 carrots, chopped into 2cm (¾ inch) chunks
400g (14oz) can of chopped tomatoes
500g (1lb 2oz) new potatoes
500ml (18fl oz) water
1 teaspoon Dijon mustard
salt and black pepper
crusty bread, to serve

FOR THE GREMOLATA
½ bunch of flat leaf parsley (about 30g/1oz), finely chopped
½ bunch of rosemary (about 30g/1oz), finely chopped
1 garlic clove, finely chopped
zest and juice of 1 lemon
salt and black pepper

Preheat the oven to 160°C (350°F), Gas Mark 4.

Pat the beef dry with kitchen paper and season with salt and pepper. Heat 1 tablespoon of the oil in a large, heavy-based, ovenproof saucepan or casserole dish (for which you have a tight-fitting lid) over a medium-high heat. When the oil is hot, add half of the beef and cook for about 2–3 minutes on each side until evenly browned. Transfer to a plate, then add the other tablespoon of oil to the pan and repeat with the remaining meat, transferring to the plate once evenly browned.

Fry the onion and celery in the remaining fat in the pan over a medium heat for 10 minutes, adding a splash more olive oil if needed. Add the garlic and herbs and fry for a minute, then add the tomato purée and fry for 1–2 minutes until a couple of shades darker. Pour in the red wine and gently scrape the bottom of the pan with a wooden spoon to lift any caramelised bits. Add the browned meat, chopped carrots, tomatoes, potatoes and measured water. Gently bring to the boil, then cover and transfer to the oven for 3 hours, checking and stirring occasionally.

Just before the stew has finished cooking, make the gremolata. Mix all the ingredients in a bowl, seasoning with salt and pepper to taste.

After 3 hours the meat should be completely tender and you should be able to pull it apart very easily with 2 forks. Remove the bay leaves and thyme, stir through the mustard and check for seasoning. Serve sprinkled with the gremolata, with crusty bread on the side.

BBQ LAMB
WITH POTATOES, SALSA VERDE & MUSTARD BEANS

SERVES 6

1 garlic bulb
2kg (4lb 8oz) leg of lamb (ask the butcher to debone and butterfly)
6 anchovies in olive oil, roughly chopped
1 bunch of rosemary, broken up
4 tablespoons olive oil
juice of 1 lemon
salt and black pepper

FOR THE POTATOES
1kg (2lb 4oz) new potatoes, roughly chopped if large
50g (1¾oz) salted butter

FOR THE SALSA VERDE
1 garlic clove, peeled
½ bunch of flat leaf parsley
½ bunch of basil
½ bunch of mint leaves
2 tablespoons capers
6 anchovies
2 teaspoons red wine vinegar
½ teaspoon Dijon mustard
100ml (3½fl oz) good-quality olive oil

FOR THE MUSTARD BEANS
400g (14oz) green beans, trimmed
1 tablespoon mustard seeds
50g (1¾oz) salted butter

WHEN SPRING DOES ITS THING AND THE SUN COMES OUT TO PLAY, WE GET THE BBQ ON BEFORE YOU CAN SAY 'GUYS, IT'S ONLY APRIL'. SERVING THE LAMB WITH SALSA VERDE KEEPS A BOUNCE IN ITS STEP, TOO. ZINGY AND DELICIOUS.

Smash the garlic cloves and discard the skins. Pierce about 15 holes all over the lamb, each about 2cm (¾ inch) deep. Stuff pieces of the garlic into the holes, followed by the anchovy pieces and rosemary sprigs. No need to be neat – just stab and shove! Drizzle the meat with half the olive oil and season well.

Place any remaining rosemary, garlic and anchovies into a roasting tin that fits the lamb snugly. Add the lemon juice and remaining olive oil. Place the lamb on top, cover the tin and leave to marinate in the fridge – ideally overnight, but an hour will do. Just make sure to remove the meat 30 minutes before cooking.

Once the meat has marinated and come to room temperature, get your BBQ or oven nice and hot. If using a BBQ, wait until it's searing hot and the coals have turned grey. If using an oven, heat to 220°C (475°F), Gas Mark 9, or to the highest setting you can.

Meanwhile, place the potatoes in a pan, cover with boiling water, add salt and cook over a medium heat for 15 minutes, until soft. Drain and return to the saucepan. Add the butter, toss to coat, then use a masher to gently crush the potatoes. Season generously with salt and pepper.

When the BBQ (or oven) is ready, cover the lamb tin with foil and place it in the middle of the grill with the lid on, or on the middle shelf of the oven, for 5 minutes. Turn, cover with foil and the lid again and cook for 5 minutes more. Remove the foil and place the lamb directly on the BBQ grill, keeping the juices in the tin. (Just keep it in the roasting tin if using an oven.) Cook for about 15 minutes, basting occasionally with the juices, then remove and pop the lamb back in the tin. Cover and let rest for 15 minutes.

To make the salsa verde, place all the ingredients into a small food processor or blender and blitz. You want a glossy, vivid green, smooth-ish sauce. Taste and adjust to your liking – we like it zingy and fresh.

For the mustard beans, place a large frying pan over a high heat (if the BBQ is still hot enough, you can use that). Add the beans and cook until charred all over,

then toss in the mustard seeds and butter. Season to taste.

Once the meat has rested, simply slice up and serve on a platter. Serve the potatoes, beans and sauce alongside in separate bowls, for everyone to help themselves. You can serve with a crisp green salad on warmer days, if you like.

Pictured overleaf ☞

SIR ROGER MOORE'S SIRLOIN STEAK

SERVES 2

2 × 300g (10½oz) good-quality
   sirloin steaks, at room
   temperature
1 tablespoon olive oil
1 teaspoon sea salt flakes

FOR THE PEPPERCORN SAUCE
2 tablespoons unsalted butter
2 shallots, peeled and finely
   chopped
1 tablespoon freshly crushed
   black peppercorns
100ml (3½fl oz) brandy
200ml (7fl oz) good-quality
   beef stock
4 tablespoons double cream

TO SERVE (OPTIONAL)
Our Perfect Chips (see page 158)
mashed potatoes
seasonal greens

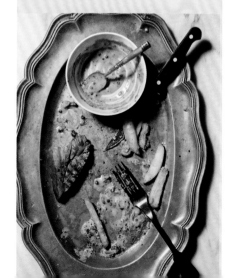

WHEN GRANDAD TONY WAS WORKING AS A CHEF AT THE CAFÉ ROYAL IN THE SIXTIES, HE SERVED ROGER MOORE A SIRLOIN STEAK FROM THE CHARCOAL GRILL. ROGER HAD HIS RARE (OF COURSE HE DID), WHICH IS, COINCIDENTALLY, EXACTLY HOW WE LIKE TO COOK OUR STEAKS NOW, WITH PEPPERCORN SAUCE AND CHIPS. GOOD CHOICE, SIR ROGER!

If you haven't already done so, remove the steaks from the fridge and bring them to room temperature.

Start by heating your BBQ. While this is getting nice and hot, make the peppercorn sauce.

For the sauce, melt the butter in a high-sided frying pan over a medium heat. Add the shallots and fry for a few minutes, then add the crushed black peppercorns. Turn up the heat and add the brandy – be careful, as it can ignite. Cook until the brandy is almost completely reduced. Add the stock and cook for about 10 minutes until reduced by two-thirds, then stir in the cream and allow the sauce to thicken slightly. Check the sauce is seasoned enough for you, then remove from the heat.

When the BBQ is nice and hot and the coals are all ashy grey, drizzle the steaks with the olive oil on both sides and season generously with the salt. Cook the steaks for around 1½ minutes on each side until they are nicely browned on the outside yet still very soft to the touch. For medium-rare, cook for about 3 minutes on each side, and for well-done, cook for 5–6 minutes on each side.

When the steaks are cooked to your liking, remove them from the grill and leave to rest for 3–4 minutes before serving.

While the steaks are resting, place the peppercorn sauce back over a low heat and give it a good mix, then pour into a jug.

Serve with chips, if you like, or a smooth, silky mash and seasonal greens. Enjoy the peppercorn sauce alongside.

easy sausage traybake

TRAYBAKES ARE A MIDWEEK SUPPER'S BEST FRIEND. SATISFYING AND EASY, YOU CAN EXPERIMENT WITH ALL SORTS OF INGREDIENTS. WE'VE PUT OUR FAVOURITE HERE, BUT TRY WHATEVER VEG NEEDS USING UP AND YOU MIGHT CREATE YOUR OWN FAVOURITE.

SERVES 6 KIDS

3 onions, peeled and cut into wedges
1 garlic bulb, cloves separated and
   halved widthways
500g (1lb 2 oz) baby new potatoes,
   halved
2 red peppers, deseeded and
   quartered
3 tablespoons olive oil
12 sausages
3 rosemary sprigs
3 thyme sprigs
400ml (14fl oz) white wine or
   chicken stock
salt and black pepper

TO SERVE
crusty bread
hot mustard (optional)

Preheat the oven to 220°C (475°F), Gas Mark 9.

Tip the onions, garlic cloves, new potatoes and peppers into a large roasting tin, then chuck in the remaining ingredients, apart from the wine or chicken stock. Season with salt and pepper and give it all a really good toss, making sure everything is well coated in the oil.

Roast for 20 minutes.

Remove from the oven and pour in the wine. Give everything a good mix and return to the oven to roast for another 20 minutes, or until the sausages are brown and the potatoes golden brown and soft when stabbed with a fork.

Serve immediately with crusty bread and some hot mustard, if you like.

valentine's feast

SERVES 2

IT SEEMS THE WAY WE LIKE TO WOO *MUST* INVOLVE FOOD! THIS VALENTINE'S FEAST IS ALL YOU WANT IT TO BE: INDULGENT, BEAUTIFUL AND FANCY. BISOUS, MES CHÉRIES!

To make the dressing for the oysters, combine the shallots and red wine vinegar in a small bowl. Separate the oyster shells using a small knife or oyster shuck (discarding any that are already open). This is actually easier than you would think and there are lots of great tutorials you can find online to help. Arrange the open oysters on a platter of ice.

To cook the lobster, bring a large pan of water to the boil (make sure it's big enough for the whole lobster to be submerged in the water). Get the lobster out the freezer and look for an indent shaped like a cross on the top of its head, then push a sharp knife down through the indent with the blade towards the front of the lobster's head (you can grip the head with the other hand and please be careful!). Add the whole lobster to the pot. Boil according to the lobster's size: 6 minutes for every 600g/1lb 5oz. Meanwhile, make the garlic butter by mixing the garlic, butter and parsley together in a small bowl. Fill a large bowl with iced water.

Preheat the grill to its highest setting. When the lobster is boiled, remove from the water and drop into the bowl of iced water to cool it down, then remove and carefully cut it in half along the back. Separate the pale, feathery objects on the inside of the lobster's body near the head and the gritty 'sand sac' just behind its eyes and discard them and then put each lobster half onto a baking sheet. Smear it all with garlic butter and grill for 2 minutes, until the butter has melted.

Drizzle the dressing over the oysters and serve in the middle of the table to share, with a dash of Tabasco and lemon wedges for squeezing on the side. Serve the lobster with Our Perfect Chips and a green salad.

FOR THE OYSTERS
2 shallots, finely chopped
100ml (3½fl oz) red wine vinegar
12 oysters in shells
Tabasco sauce, to taste
1 lemon, cut into wedges

FOR THE LOBSTER
1 lobster (put in the freezer
    10 minutes before cooking to
    stun it; note its weight)
3 garlic cloves, crushed
100g (3½oz) butter, softened
bunch of parsley, very finely
    chopped
Out Perfect Chips (see page 158),
    to serve
green salad, to serve

TIP
GET YOURSELF A SEAFOOD PICK AND LOBSTER CRACKER TO GET THE DELICIOUS LOBSTER MEAT FROM THE CLAWS AND SHELLS.

RICHARD 'PIE ON THE STAIRS' JONES

SERVES 6

THIS STEAK AND GUINNESS PIE IS FROM WHEN RICHARD WAS ABOUT SIX AND HELPING HIS DAD IN THE KITCHEN AT THE HOTEL WHERE HE WAS CHEF. LITTLE RICHARD WAS HEADING DOWN THE STAIRS TO DELIVER THE PIE TO THE BAR, BUT SLIPPED, CAUSING THE PIE TO GO EVERYWHERE, AND EARNING THE NICKNAME RICHARD 'PIE ON THE STAIRS' JONES WITH THE LOCALS. THEY STILL CALL HIM THAT TO THIS DAY (PROBABLY).

4 tablespoons olive oil, plus extra for greasing
1kg (2lb 4oz) good-quality rump steak, chopped into bite-sized pieces
200g (7oz) button mushrooms, finely chopped
2 large onions, finely chopped
2 large celery sticks, roughly chopped
1 garlic bulb, cloves peeled
3 tablespoons plain flour, plus extra for dusting
4 thyme sprigs
4 bay leaves
300–400ml (10–14fl oz) beef stock
300ml (10fl oz) Guinness
1 tablespoon Worcestershire sauce
1 tablespoon English mustard
320g (11½oz) shortcrust pastry (store-bought)
320g (11½oz) ready-rolled puff pastry (store-bought)
1 large free-range egg, beaten
salt and black pepper

Preheat the oven to 160°C (350°F), Gas Mark 4.

Start with the pie filling. Put the olive oil in a large ovenproof casserole dish set over a high heat. Season the steak with plenty of salt and pepper, then fry it in batches until evenly browned. Transfer to a large plate and set aside. Add the mushrooms to the casserole and fry for 5 minutes, stirring frequently, then add the onions, celery and garlic cloves and fry for 10 minutes, stirring frequently to ensure nothing burns. Return the steak to the casserole along with any meat juices, stir in the flour and thyme and fry for a further minute. Add the bay leaves, 300ml (10fl oz) of the stock, Guinness, Worcestershire sauce and mustard, season with salt and pepper, and bring to the boil.

Transfer the casserole to the oven and cook with the lid on for 1½ hours, checking that the pie filling hasn't reduced too much after 1 hour. If it's starting to look dry, add a little extra stock.

Remove from the oven and ladle the mixture out onto a baking tray (to cool down quickly). Turn the oven up to 200°C (425°F), Gas Mark 7, and place a large baking tray on the bottom of the oven to heat up. Grease your pie dish with a little olive oil.

While the filling is cooling, roll out the shortcrust pastry to 4mm (¼-inch) thick on a lightly flour-dusted work surface until it is large enough to line your pie dish or tin (we use a 30cm/12 inch round pie dish). Drape the pastry into the dish, leaving about 3cm (1 inch) of overhanging pastry (if you have any more than this, trim it off). Place the dish in the fridge until the filling is cooled.

When the filling is cool enough, bake the shortcrust pie base for 5 minutes with some spoons or baking beads in the middle to hold it down. Remove from the oven and transfer the cooled filling to the pastry-lined pie dish (removing the spoons first!)

For the pie lid, unroll the sheet of puff pastry. Crack the egg into a small bowl and give it a little mix with a fork, then use a pastry brush to brush a little egg around the lip of the shortcrust pastry. Place the puff pastry on top, press together to seal, then trim away the excess pastry. Pinch to crimp the pastry all around the edge. Cut a small cross in the centre of the pastry lid to allow steam to escape, then evenly brush the top of the pie with the egg wash.

Place the pie on the preheated baking tray on the bottom of the oven and bake for 30–35 minutes, or until the pastry is golden and crisp.

We serve ours with peas, baked beans, extra gravy, crusty bread or mashed potato (with a little mustard mixed in). Our Perfect Chips (see page 158) work with this too.

TIP
IF YOU WANT TO SERVE THIS WITH GRAVY, WHEN MAKING THE PIE FILLING TRANSFER SOME OF THE THICKENED SAUCE TO A PAN, ADD MORE STOCK AND REDUCE OVER A MEDIUM HEAT.

CHOCOLATE CITRUS PANETTONE BREAD & BUTTER PUDDING

THIS IS A HYBRID – A CLASSIC BRITISH PUDDING WITH AN ITALIAN TWIST, REPLACING THE BREAD WITH DELICIOUS CAKEY PANETTONE. WE LIKE TO SERVE OURS WITH A GOOD DRIZZLE OF EXTRA CREAM, BUT IT'S EQUALLY AS GOOD WITH A SCOOP OF VANILLA ICE CREAM.

SERVES 6

150g (5½oz) salted butter, plus extra for greasing
3 tablespoons demerara sugar
1kg (2lb 4 oz) panettone, sliced into 3cm (1¼ inch) slices
350ml (12fl oz) double cream, plus extra to serve
300ml (10fl oz) milk
1 teaspoon vanilla bean paste
3 large free-range eggs, plus 3 large free-range egg yolks
100g (3½oz) golden caster sugar
grated zest of 1 orange
grated zest of 1 lemon
100g (3½oz) good-quality dark chocolate, roughly broken into shards
double cream, to serve

Preheat the oven to 180°C (400°F), Gas Mark 6.

Grease a 28cm (11 inch) loose-bottomed tart tin with a little butter. Tip 1 tablespoon of the demerara sugar into the tin and bash it all about so it evenly covers the base and sides of the tin.

Use about 4 slices of panettone to line the tart tin. You'll need to squash and move it about to create a panettone tart case, so just squish it into the tin, tearing extra bits of panettone to fill gaps, if needed. Set aside.

Pour the cream, milk and vanilla bean paste into a medium saucepan, add the butter and place over a low heat. Simmer for 5 minutes.

Crack the eggs into a large bowl, add the extra egg yolks, and whisk lightly. Add the golden caster sugar and whisk together for a few minutes. Still whisking constantly, pour in the hot cream mixture until well combined. Add the orange and lemon zests and give it another mix.

Pour one-third of the custard mixture into the panettone tart case and leave to soak in.

Tear the remaining panettone into rough strips – you don't need to worry too much about size and shape. Tumble half of the panettone strips into the tart case, then cover with about half of the remaining custard. Stab about half of the chocolate shards in randomly, then cover with the remaining panettone strips and the remaining custard. Finish with the last of the chocolate and sprinkle over the remaining 2 tablespoons of demerara sugar.

Bake for 20–25 minutes, or until just set.

Remove from the oven and leave to cool for 10 minutes before serving with double cream.

EUROPEAN HOLIDAY♥ FAVOURITES

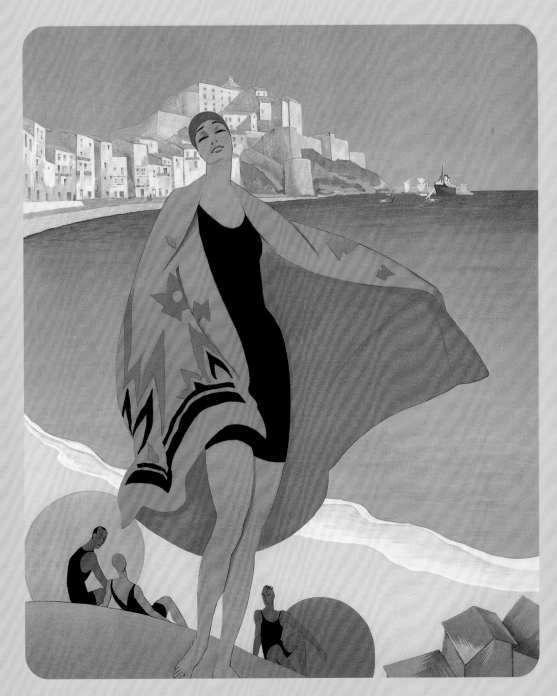

Aren't we so lucky to be part of the European continent? From Russian borscht to Spanish tortilla, we love it all. It's amazing that we can explore so many different regions and flavours without going too far. It's a big part of our job as musicians to travel, so we've done our best to bring our favourites home to our table, and now we want to share them with you.

SPAGHETTI VONGOLE

ONE OF OUR ALL-TIME FAVOURITE DISHES, THIS LOOKS FANCY, TASTES DECADENT AND IS SURPRISINGLY SIMPLE TO COOK. THIS DISH IS VERY QUICK, SO GET ALL YOUR PREP DONE BEFORE YOU START COOKING.

SERVES 4–6

1kg (2lb 4oz) small clams, scrubbed clean (discard any that aren't tightly closed)
4 banana shallots, finely sliced
6 garlic cloves, finely sliced
1 bunch of flat leaf parsley, stems finely sliced and leaves roughly chopped
15 cherry tomatoes, quartered
450g (1lb) dried spaghetti
150ml (5fl oz) extra-virgin olive oil
juice of 1 lemon
350ml (12fl oz) white wine
salt and black pepper

TO SERVE
warm bread
Simple Italian Chilli Oil
(optional, see page 89)

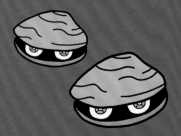

Place a large pan of water over a high heat, season well with salt. Scrub the clams and chop the veg and herbs as instructed opposite.

Add the spaghetti to the boiling water and cook according to the packet instructions. After about 2 minutes start the sauce.

Put the olive oil in your largest pan with a lid and place over a medium heat. Add the shallots and garlic and fry until lightly golden, about 3 minutes.

Add the parsley stems and cherry tomatoes. Squeeze in the juice of the lemon and fry for a further minute. Pour in half the white wine and cook for a few minutes, until the wine has evaporated.

Tip in the cleaned clams and the remaining wine. It will splutter, so be careful. Give everything a good shake and pop the lid on. After 3–4 minutes the clams will start to open. Keep shaking the pan around until all of them have opened.

Remove the pan from the heat and discard any clams that haven't yet opened.

Your pasta should be perfectly al dente now so drain and chuck in with the clams. Add the parsley leaves and season well with salt and pepper to taste. Serve with warm bread and chilli oil for those who want it.

a TRIO OF PERFECT SALADS

EACH SERVES 4–6

SALADS ARE ONE OF OUR FAVOURITE THINGS. SERIOUSLY! THEY CAN BE PACKED FULL OF EXCITING FLAVOURS AND TASTE SO FULL OF CRUNCH AND LIFE. HERE'S SOME WE ADD TO BBQS OR TO A NICE PIECE OF FISH.

OUR FAVE TOMATO SALAD

2 banana shallots, finely sliced
1 garlic clove, crushed
1 teaspoon golden caster sugar
1 tablespoon red wine vinegar
2 tablespoons good-quality olive oil
1kg (2lb 4oz) mixed tomatoes, roughly chopped
1 ball of burrata (about 150g/5½oz)
handful of basil leaves
salt and black pepper

Place the shallots, garlic and sugar in a serving bowl. Drizzle over the red wine vinegar and olive oil, then toss it all together. Toss the tomatoes in with the shallot dressing. Pop the burrata in the middle, season well with salt and pepper, scatter over the basil leaves and serve.

RAW COURGETTE SALAD

75g (2½oz) pine nuts
5 mixed-colour courgettes
100ml (3½fl oz) extra-virgin olive oil
zest and juice of 1 lemon
1 teaspoon honey
handful of flat leaf parsley leaves
100g (3½oz) Parmesan cheese, grated (optional)
salt and black pepper
1 fresh red chilli, to serve (optional)

Toast the pine nuts in a dry frying pan until golden brown. Watch them carefully, as they are quick to burn. Tip out into a serving bowl.

Slice all the courgettes lengthways on a mandoline or with a veg peeler, stopping when you get to the seedy core. Place the courgette ribbons in the serving bowl and add all the remaining salad ingredients. Toss together. Season well with salt and pepper and serve with chopped red chilli on the side, if you like.

SHAVED FENNEL SALAD

4 fennel bulbs
zest and juice of 1 lemon
1 teaspoon sea salt flakes
2 tablespoons extra-virgin olive oil
1 chicory head, roughly sliced
½ bunch of flat leaf parsley, leaves picked

Using a sharp knife or a mandoline, finely slice the fennel into lengths, then tip onto a large serving platter or bowl. Sprinkle over the lemon zest and juice. Season with the salt, drizzle over the oil, add the chicory and toss together. Scatter over the parsley leaves and serve.

Pictured overleaf ☞

caramelised pepper pasta

SERVES 4

100ml (3½fl oz) extra-virgin
     olive oil
1 onion, finely sliced
4 garlic cloves, finely sliced
6 peppers, deseeded and sliced into
     3cm (1¼ inch) strips
1 tablespoon red wine vinegar
300g (10½oz) dried rigatoni or
     penne pasta
2 tablespoons capers
handful of flat leaf parsley leaves
salt and black pepper

TO SERVE (OPTIONAL)
grated Parmesan cheese (or any
     cheese of your choice)
a drizzle of Simple Italian Chilli Oil
     (see page 89)

KIT'S FAVOURITE HOME-COOKED SAUCE. THE LONGER
YOU COOK THE PEPPERS, THE BETTER, THEY KNOW WHAT
TO DO AND BECOME THE MOST GORGEOUS FLAVOURFUL
THING EVER. THE BEST BITS CAN GET STUCK TO THE PAN
SO MAKE SURE YOU GET IT ALL!

Heat the olive oil in a large frying pan over a low heat. Add the onion,
garlic and peppers to the pan and turn the heat up to medium. Fry for
25–30 minutes, stirring often to ensure nothing catches and burns,
until the onions and peppers are completely soft and caramelised.
After 15 minutes of this time, add the red wine vinegar and season
with salt and pepper.

Meanwhile, fill a large pan with well-salted water and bring to the
boil. Add the pasta and cook until al dente.

Drain the pasta and add to the pepper mixture, then toss in the
capers and parsley leaves and mix to combine.

Serve with a grating of Parmesan and a drizzle of Simple Italian Chilli
Oil, if you like.

parmigiana

SERVES 6

AN ITALIAN CLASSIC AND HEARTY FAMILY VEGETARIAN FAVOURITE, PERFECT FOR
COMMUNAL MIDWEEK FEASTING. ONE OF THOSE MEALS THAT'S MADE WITH LOVE, SO WELL
WORTH GOING THE EXTRA MILE AND MAKING IT YOURSELF.

FOR THE TOMATO SAUCE
olive oil
4 garlic cloves, finely sliced
3 × 400g cans of good-quality
    plum tomatoes

FOR THE AUBERGINES
100ml (3½fl oz) olive oil
juice of 1 lemon
3 garlic cloves, finely sliced
1 heaped tablespoon dried oregano
5 large aubergines, trimmed and
    sliced lengthways into 1cm
    (½ inch) slices
salt and black pepper

Preheat the oven to 180°C (400°F), Gas Mark 6.

Start with the tomato sauce. Set a large pan with a lid over a medium
heat and pour in enough olive oil to cover the bottom of the pan.
Add the garlic and fry until golden brown, then add the tomatoes
(be careful, as the tomatoes will spit). Cover with the lid and simmer for
20 minutes, or until the sauce is thickened and reduced.

Meanwhile, get on with the aubergines. Preheat a griddle pan over a
high heat, or you can also do this on a BBQ, if you like.

Put the olive oil, lemon juice, sliced garlic and oregano in a deep baking
tray, mix to combine and season generously with salt and pepper.

Working in batches, place a single layer of aubergine slices onto the
griddle (or BBQ) and char on each side until each slice has deep black
griddle lines and is starting to soften. Transfer the charred aubergine
slices to the oil mixture in the tray and toss to coat. Continue until all
the aubergine slices are charred and coated in oil.

TO FINISH
100g (3½oz) vegetarian Parmesan-
   style cheese, grated
2 × 125g (4½oz) balls of mozzarella,
   sliced
1 bunch of basil
2 handfuls of dried breadcrumbs
½ bunch of oregano, leaves picked
   and finely chopped
3 tablespoons olive oil

TO SERVE (OPTIONAL)
dressed rocket leaves
focaccia

Spoon a layer of the tomato sauce into a 25 × 15cm (10 × 6 inch) high-sided baking dish, then add a scattering of Parmesan-style cheese and tear some of the mozzarella slices in random chunks all over. Add a single layer of aubergines and a few basil leaves on top. Repeat these layers until you've used up all the ingredients but still have a few slices of mozzarella left, finishing with a little sauce and another good sprinkling of Parmesan-style cheese.

Toss the breadcrumbs together with the oregano and olive oil, then sprinkle the mixture on top of the parmigiana. Tear over the remaining mozzarella. Bake for 45 minutes, or until golden and crisp.

Leave to cool for 5 minutes before slicing and serving. We like to serve this with some simply dressed rocket leaves and some focaccia for mopping up the sauce.

JeLena's TORTILLa
WITH CHORIZO a La SIDRa

OUR AU PAIR JELENA IS AN INSTINCTIVE, UNFLAPPABLE COOK. SHE CAN LOOK IN THE FRIDGE AND WHERE I SEE NOTHING, SHE SEES A MEAL. LUCKY KIDS… WELL ACTUALLY, LUCKY US. JELENA WAS A REFUGEE FROM SERBIA WHEN SHE ARRIVED IN SPAIN AGED NINE. NOW SHE COOKS SPANISH FOOD FOR US ALL THE TIME AND THIS TORTILLA DOESN'T LAST LONG IN OUR HOME. IT'S THAT GOOD. WE OFTEN PAIR IT WITH THIS DELICIOUS SIDE DISH – CHORIZO A LA SIDRA (CHORIZO IN CIDER). IF YOU'VE NEVER TRIED IT BEFORE, YOU'RE GONNA LOVE IT!

SERVES 4

100ml (3½fl oz) olive oil
1 large onion, finely sliced
2 garlic cloves, peeled
1kg (2lb 4oz) potatoes
    (we use Maris Piper, but
    you could use russets),
    peeled and chopped into
    2cm (¾inch) chunks
6 large free-range eggs, plus
    1 free-range egg yolk
salt and black pepper
bread, to serve (optional)

**FOR THE CHORIZO
A LA SIDRA**
1 tablespoon olive oil
500g (1lb 2oz) cured or
    semi-cured Spanish
    chorizo, sliced
1 red pepper, sliced
225ml (8fl oz) apple cider,
    or any fruity cider
4 bay leaves
400g (14oz) can of
    chopped tomatoes

Start with making the chorizo a la sidra. Preheat the oven to 180°C (400°F), Gas Mark 6. Put the olive oil and chorizo in a frying pan and cook over a medium-high heat until crispy, about 10 minutes. Remove the chorizo from the pan, retaining the oil, and cook the pepper until soft, about 5 minutes. Return the chorizo to the pan, add the cider and allow to cook for 5 minutes. Add the bay leaves and tomatoes and cook for a further 5 minutes, seasoning to taste. Transfer the mixture to a small baking dish and cook in the oven for 10 minutes until caramelised.

To make the tortilla, pour the olive oil into a medium nonstick frying pan and set over a medium heat, then add the onion and garlic and fry until soft but not coloured. Remove the garlic cloves and add the potato chunks. Cook, stirring occasionally, for about 20 minutes until the potatoes are cooked through. Keep an eye on it to ensure that nothing catches and burns.

Crack the eggs and the additional egg yolk into a mixing bowl and season well with salt and pepper.

Pour the eggs over the potatoes and turn the heat down to low. Give everything a good mix, then leave to cook for 6–8 minutes, or until just firm and coloured on the bottom.

Carefully pop a plate over the top of the pan and, using a quick flipping motion, flip the tortilla onto the plate. Slide the tortilla back into the pan and cook for a further 3 minutes over a medium heat. We like ours a little runny in the middle, but continue to cook if you like yours a little more set.

Serve the tortilla with the chorizo, with bread on the side if you like.

(IT'S NOT) PAELLA

SERVES 6

100ml (3½fl oz) olive oil
300g (10½oz) cooking chorizo, roughly chopped into 3cm (1¼ inch) chunks
1 onion, finely sliced
4 garlic cloves, finely sliced
1 heaped teaspoon smoked paprika
300g (10½oz) paella rice
large pinch of saffron strands
750ml (generous 1¼ pints) chicken stock
230g jar of roasted red peppers, drained and cut into strips
1 bunch of flat leaf parsley: stalks finely chopped, leaves roughly torn
250g (9oz) large peeled raw prawns
200g (7oz) mussels, cleaned (discard any that are not closed)
zest and juice of 1 lemon
100g (3½oz) frozen peas
salt and black pepper

TO SERVE
1 lemon, chopped into wedges
aïoli (optional, see page 56 for homemade)

WE FIRST COOKED THIS A FEW YEARS AGO AND POSTED IT ONLINE AS 'PAELLA'. YES, WE KNOW IT'S NOT PAELLA. BUT IT'S BASED ON THAT AND IT'S REALLY GOOD. HAVE A GO AT THIS MEAL IF YOU WANT SOMETHING THAT'S NOT PAELLA, BUT KIND OF THINKS IT IS.

Pour the olive oil into your largest frying pan or paella pan and set over a medium heat. Chuck in the chorizo and cook for a few minutes or until starting to colour and crisp. Add the onion, garlic and paprika and fry for about 8 minutes until the onion is soft. Add the rice and fry for a few minutes, stirring continuously.

Add the saffron strands to the stock, then pour the stock into the pan. Cover with a snug-fitting lid or some foil and simmer for 25 minutes.

Remove the lid or foil and add the peppers, parsley stalks, prawns, mussels, lemon zest and juice and the frozen peas. Stir well, cover with a lid again or re-cover with the foil, and cook for a further 10 minutes.

Remove the lid or foil and discard any mussels that haven't opened by this stage. Season well with salt and pepper, and scatter over the parsley leaves.

Serve with the lemon wedges on the side. We like to eat ours with lots of aïoli and a crisp wine for the adults.

a CLASSIC SPAGHETTI BOLOGNESE

HERE WE HAVE TWO VERSIONS: SLOWER FROM HIM, QUICKER FROM HER. LOTS OF PEOPLE GROW UP WITH THIS BEING PART OF THE FAMILY MENU, AND THIS IS HOW WE DO OURS.

SERVES 6

1 tablespoon olive oil
4 garlic cloves, finely chopped
1 onion, finely chopped
2 carrots, finely chopped
2 celery sticks, finely chopped
2 rosemary sprigs, finely chopped
6 dry-cured, higher-welfare, smoked streaky bacon rashers, roughly chopped
500g (1lb 2oz) minced beef
500g (1lb 2oz) minced pork
1 teaspoon fennel seeds
400ml (14fl oz) red wine
2 tablespoons tomato purée
2 × 400g (14oz) cans of plum tomatoes
juice of 1 lemon
500g (1lb 2oz) dried spaghetti
salt and black pepper

TO SERVE
basil leaves
grated Parmesan cheese
garlic bread (optional)

Heat the olive oil in a large heavy-based casserole dish or pan over a medium heat, add the veg and the rosemary and fry for 10 minutes, or until soft and translucent. Add the bacon, increase the heat and fry for a further 5 minutes. Scoop out the mixture into a bowl and set aside.

Add the minced beef and pork to the pan and break up with a wooden spoon. Fry over a high heat for 5 minutes, or until starting to brown, then season well with salt and pepper and add the fennel seeds. Pour in the wine, then return the veg mixture to the pan and stir well. Add the tomato purée and canned tomatoes and squeeze in the lemon juice.

Cover with a lid, then cook over a medium-low heat for 2 hours, stirring every 30 minutes.

About 15 minutes before the time is up on the sauce, bring a large pan of well-salted water to the boil over a high heat. Add the spaghetti and cook according to the packet instructions.

Drain the cooked spaghetti or use tongs to transfer it straight into the sauce. Mix gently, adding a little of the pasta cooking water to loosen it up, if needed.

Top with basil leaves and a grating of Parmesan before serving. Our kids love a little warm garlic bread with theirs, to mop up the sauce.

SOPHIE'S QUICK VERSION

FRY CHOPPED GARLIC AND ONION UNTIL TRANSPARENT, THEN ADD MINCED BEEF AND BROWN OFF. ADD 2 CANS OF CHOPPED TOMATOES, TOMATO PURÉE, A LITTLE SQUEEZE OF HONEY, A STOCK CUBE, SALT AND PEPPER, A LITTLE SPLASH OF WORCESTERSHIRE SAUCE AND SOME CHOPPED CARROTS (OR GRATED IF THE KIDS AREN'T TOO KEEN – WORKS WITH MINE!). I ALSO TEAR SOME MUSHROOMS IN, IF I HAVE ANY. IT'S NICE TO LET IT ALL COOK FOR AN HOUR, SO THE SAUCE REDUCES AND INTENSIFIES, BUT IT WILL BE TASTY IN 30 MINUTES IF YOU HAVEN'T GOT BUCKETLOADS OF TIME.

OUR FAVOURITE FISH STEW WITH HOMEMADE AÏOLI

THIS IS A VERY SATISFYING DISH AND THE EXTRA FLAVOUR AND FLAIR OF THE AÏOLI BRINGS THE WHOLE THING TO LIFE.

SERVES 4-6

3 tablespoons extra-virgin olive oil
1 bunch of flat leaf parsley: stems finely chopped; leaves torn
1 large onion, finely chopped
3 celery sticks, finely chopped
1 head of fennel, finely chopped
3 garlic cloves, roughly chopped
zest and juice of 1 lemon
1 teaspoon chilli flakes, or to taste
2 × 400g cans of chopped tomatoes
300ml (10fl oz) white wine
400ml (14fl oz) fish stock
1 tablespoon tomato purée
pinch of saffron (optional)
250g (9oz) skinless halibut fillet
250g (9oz) skinless salmon fillet
12 large prawns, peeled, deveined
250g (9oz) mussels or clams (discard any that are not closed)
salt and black pepper

FOR THE AÏOLI
2 free-range egg yolks
500ml (18fl oz) sunflower oil
1–2 tablespoons white wine vinegar
1 heaped teaspoon Dijon mustard
2 garlic cloves
juice of 1 lemon
paprika (optional)
salt and black pepper

TO SERVE
toasted sourdough slices
lemon wedges

Heat 2 tablespoons of the oil in a large heavy-based pan that has a lid over a medium heat. Add the chopped parsley stems, chopped vegetables and garlic and fry for 10 minutes, stirring often to ensure it doesn't catch on the bottom of the pan. Add the lemon zest and chilli flakes and fry for a further minute. Add the tomatoes, wine, stock, tomato purée and saffron, if using, and season well with salt and pepper. Bring to the boil, then reduce the heat to medium and simmer, uncovered, for 15 minutes.

Meanwhile, get on with the aïoli. Whisk the egg yolks in a bowl, gradually adding half the oil as you mix. This should be done slowly until it starts to thicken, about 5 minutes. Then whisk the vinegar in, which will loosen the mixture a little and it will become paler. Add the remaining oil as you continue to whisk, then season with the mustard and a pinch of salt. (Alternatively, you can skip this and use your favourite shop-bought mayonnaise.) Grate the garlic cloves into the mayo and squeeze in the lemon juice (add a little paprika if you like a bit of spice). Season to taste and scoop into a bowl.

Chop the fish into bite-sized pieces and add to the tomato sauce along with the majority of the lemon juice. Cover the pan with the lid and simmer gently for 3 minutes. Add the prawns and simmer for a further 2 minutes, then add the mussels or clams, put the lid on the pan and cook for a further 5–6 minutes until the shells have opened.

Stir in half of the parsley leaves and taste, adjusting the seasoning if needed. Scatter over the remaining parsley and the remaining lemon juice and drizzle over the remaining tablespoon of olive oil. Serve alongside the aïoli and toasted sourdough with a lemon wedge on the side.

THE PERFECT VEGGIE RISOTTO FOR ALL

THIS ONE IS ALL ABOUT VEG PREP – CHOPPING THE VEGETABLES AS SMALL AS POSSIBLE, SO THEY COOK QUICKLY AND ARE EASILY HIDDEN FROM BEADY LITTLE EYES.

SERVES 4

- 100g (3½oz) dried porcini mushrooms
- 1 litre (1¾ pints) vegetable stock
- 4 tablespoons olive oil
- ½ butternut squash, deseeded and finely chopped
- 3 celery sticks, finely chopped
- 2 carrots, finely chopped
- 4 shallots, finely chopped
- 4 garlic cloves, finely chopped
- handful of sage leaves
- juice of 1 lemon
- 300g (10½oz) arborio risotto rice
- 300ml (10fl oz) dry white wine
- 60g (2¼oz) butter, chopped into pieces
- 100g (3½oz) vegetarian Parmesan-style cheese, grated, plus extra to serve
- salt and black pepper

Boil the kettle. Place the mushrooms in a heatproof bowl, pour in enough boiling water to cover (about 200ml/7fl oz) and set aside to soften for about 15 minutes.

Pour the stock into a saucepan and place it over a medium heat, keeping it at a simmer at all times. Drain the mushroom soaking liquid into the stock. Finely chop the soaked mushrooms and set aside.

Heat the olive oil in a large heavy-based saucepan over a medium heat. Add all the chopped vegetables, sage and mushrooms and fry for 10 minutes. When the veg is golden, add the lemon juice and fry for a further 5 minutes until the veg is soft, stirring frequently.

Add the rice and toast for a couple of minutes or until the rice has turned slightly translucent, then pour in the wine and stir continuously until completely absorbed. Start adding the stock, a ladleful at a time, and continue to stir until the stock has been absorbed. This should take about 15 minutes.

Beat in the butter and Parmesan-style cheese and season to taste. Cover the pan and turn off the heat, then leave to sit for 2 minutes.

Remove the lid, stir the risotto and ladle into bowls. Top with a little extra cheese to serve.

COD & CHORIZO STEW

WE ADORE THIS STEW. IT'S QUICK TO MAKE BUT FULL OF FLAVOUR (AND TASTES EVEN BETTER AS LEFTOVERS THE NEXT DAY). A STEW THAT'S FOR ALL YEAR ROUND, NOT JUST WHEN IT'S COLD OUTSIDE.

SERVES 4

2 tablespoons olive oil
200g (7oz) cooking chorizo, chopped into bite-sized chunks
1 large onion, roughly chopped
3 garlic cloves, finely sliced
2 celery sticks, chopped
2 red peppers, deseeded and chopped
1 teaspoon coriander seeds
1 teaspoon fennel seeds
400ml (14fl oz) red wine
1 tablespoon tomato purée
2 × 400g (14oz) cans of chopped tomatoes
½ teaspoon dried chilli flakes
200g (7oz) couscous
1 vegetable stock cube
300ml (10fl oz) boiling water
400g (14oz) cod fillets
½ bunch of flat leaf parsley leaves
1 lemon, cut into wedges
salt and black pepper

Heat the olive oil in a large pan over a medium heat and chuck in the chorizo. Fry for a few minutes or until it starts to release a little of its oil, then add the onion and garlic and fry for a further 5 minutes. Add the celery and peppers, along with the coriander and fennel seeds and fry for a further 5 minutes. Pour in the wine and let it evaporate a little, then add the tomato purée, chopped tomatoes and dried chilli flakes and season with salt and pepper.

Meanwhile, bring the kettle to the boil.

Place the couscous in a medium mixing bowl. Pop the stock cube into a measuring jug and pour over the measured boiling water, then give it a good mix. Pour 200ml (7fl oz) of the stock over the couscous and cover or place a lid on top. Leave to steam for 5–8 minutes.

Pour the remaining stock into the tomato pan and bring to the boil. Carefully nestle the cod fillets into the sauce so they are mostly covered, then pop a lid on the pan and simmer for 5 minutes.

Fluff the couscous with a fork.

When the fish is lovely and flaky, serve the stew with a sprinkle of parsley leaves, with lemon wedges and some fluffy couscous on the side.

SOPHIE'S BORSCHT

SERVES 6

olive oil

1kg (2lb 4oz) oxtail

2 large onions, chopped into
   bite-sized pieces

4 bay leaves

1.5 litres (2½ pints) good-quality
   beef stock

5 raw beetroot, chopped into 1cm
   (½ inch) pieces

4 carrots, sliced into 1cm
   (½ inch) pieces

2 large waxy potatoes, chopped into
   1cm (½ inch) pieces

½ Savoy cabbage, finely shredded

3 tablespoons red wine vinegar

1 large bunch of dill, finely chopped

salt and black pepper

150g (5½oz) soured cream, to serve

EVERY TIME WE GO TO EASTERN EUROPE, WE HAVE TO EAT BORSCHT: THIS UKRANIAN-INSPIRED VERSION IS AMAZINGLY NOURISHING, ALWAYS DELICIOUS AND THE BEST COLOUR YOU COULD HOPE FOR IN A BOWL.

Place a large casserole dish or pan over a high heat, add enough olive oil to lightly cover the bottom and add the oxtail. Brown the meat evenly, turning it every couple of minutes. Add the onions to the pan along with the bay leaves and stir well to combine. Pour in the beef stock and bring to the boil, then reduce the heat to a simmer, cover and cook for roughly 4 hours until the meat is falling off the bone.

Meanwhile, preheat the oven to 180°C (400°F), Gas Mark 6. Throw the beetroot, carrots and potatoes into a large roasting pan, drizzle with olive oil, season well with salt and pepper and toss to coat the veg. Roast for 40–45 minutes, tossing halfway through.

When ready, transfer the beef to a chopping board. Pull the meat off the bone and chop into small (3cm/1¼ inch) chunks. Discard the bones.

Skim any excess fat from the top of the cooking broth and return the pan to a medium heat. Tip in the roasted vegetables, meat, cabbage, red wine vinegar and half of the dill, bring back to a simmer and cook for a further 20 minutes.

Taste and season with salt and plenty of freshly cracked black pepper. Serve ladled into bowls, with a good dollop of soured cream and a sprinkling of the remaining dill.

SERVES 6

JONES FAMILY VEGETABLE LASAGNE

THIS WAS A REGULAR DISH ON THE TABLE IN THE JONES HOUSEHOLD BACK IN THE EIGHTIES AND WE LIKE TO MAKE IT FOR OUR SMALL JONES BOYS NOW.

7 tablespoons olive oil

2 onions, finely chopped

4 garlic cloves, finely chopped

1 courgette, chopped

1 aubergine, chopped

300g (10½oz) mixed mushrooms, cleaned, roughly chopped

1 tablespoon dried oregano

½ teaspoon dried chilli flakes

juice of 1 lemon

2 × 400g (14oz) cans of chopped tomatoes

12 dried lasagne sheets

4 large tomatoes, sliced

100g (3½oz) vegetarian Parmesan-style cheese, freshly grated

salt and black pepper

FOR THE CHEESE SAUCE

100g (3½oz) butter

100g (3½oz) plain flour

750ml (generous 1¼ pints) full-fat milk (or milk of your choice)

200g (7oz) mature Cheddar cheese, grated

100g (3½oz) mozzarella cheese, grated

1 teaspoon Dijon mustard

salt and black pepper

TO SERVE

green salad

garlic bread

Preheat the oven to 200°C (425°F), Gas Mark 7.

Heat half of the olive oil in a large frying pan over a high heat, then add the onions and fry. After 3 minutes, add the garlic and fry for 2 more minutes, then add the rest of the vegetables and fry for a further 10 minutes, stirring as you go until they catch a little. Add the oregano and chilli flakes and fry for a further minute, then squeeze in the lemon juice and season with salt and pepper. Add the canned tomatoes and leave to simmer for 30 minutes.

Meanwhile, make the sauce. Melt the butter in a large saucepan over a medium heat. Add the flour and mix in well, then cook for a couple of minutes, stirring continuously with a wooden spoon. Gradually whisk in the milk, bit by bit, ensuring you beat out any lumps as you go, until the sauce is smooth, thick and silky. Add the cheeses and the mustard and season to taste. Continue to cook the sauce for a further 5 minutes, stirring. Remove from the heat.

When the veg is cooked, you can start building the lasagne. Place a layer of half the pasta sheets on the bottom of a 39 × 25cm (15½ × 10 inch) roasting tray, then spoon in a layer of veg, followed by a layer of cheese sauce. Continue the layering once more, finishing with a layer of the sauce. Place the sliced tomatoes on top, followed by the Parmesan-style cheese.

Bake for 40–45 minutes, or until golden and bubbling.

Serve with a green salad and garlic bread.

OUR WEDDING TIRAMISU

WE GOT MARRIED IN ITALY AND I THINK 90 PER CENT OF THE
DECISION TO WED THERE WAS THE FACT IT MEANT ITALIAN
FOOD FOR THE WEDDING. TIRAMISU IS OUR KIND OF PUDDING
– SWEET BUT NOT TOO SWEET, CREAMY BUT NOT TOO CREAMY
AND LIGHT ENOUGH TO HAVE SECONDS. PLEASE.

SERVES 8

2 free-range eggs, separated
100g (3½oz) caster sugar
450g (1lb) mascarpone cheese
1 teaspoon vanilla bean paste
150ml (5fl oz) double cream
a squeeze of fresh lemon juice
**300ml (10fl oz) freshly brewed
  coffee (warm, not hot)**
100ml (3½fl oz) dessert wine
**200g (7oz) Savoiardi biscuits or
  sponge fingers**
**50g (1¾oz) hazelnut chocolate,
  finely grated**
cacao nibs (optional)

Separate the egg whites and yolks into 2 large mixing bowls.

Add half the sugar to the egg yolks and whisk until smooth and a
little paler in colour. Add the mascarpone and vanilla bean paste and
whisk until smooth. Pour in the cream and continue to whisk until it is
completely incorporated.

Squeeze a little lemon juice into the egg whites and whisk until you have
soft peaks. You can do this by hand or use an electric whisk. Fold the egg
whites into the mascarpone mixture and mix until well incorporated.

Pour the warm coffee into a shallow dish along with the dessert wine
and the remaining sugar.

Place 2 dollops of the mascarpone mixture in a 25 × 15cm (10 × 6 inch)
dish, and swirl it around to cover the base of the dish.

Soak a few sponge fingers in the coffee mixture for 10 seconds, or
until a little soft but not falling apart. Layer the soaked fingers on top
of the mascarpone layer and continue with this soaking and layering
process, until all the ingredients are used up, finishing with a layer of the
mascarpone mixture. Top with the grated hazelnut chocolate and cacao
nibs to finish.

Chill in the fridge for 1 hour before serving. You can also make this ahead
and keep it in the fridge overnight.

TASTY♥ MIDWEEK MIDDLE eastern

Our favourite local restaurant is a Turkish one called Lara, which has been in the area since the Seventies. This chapter is a tribute to it and to our trips to that region. Such a wonderful mix of flavours and dishes that always look inviting on your plate, too.

CHICKEN, COUSCOUS & PRESERVED LEMON BAKE

SERVES 4

4 chicken breasts, skin-on, sliced
   into large pieces
2 preserved lemons, finely chopped
2 teaspoons dried chilli flakes
½ teaspoon ground cinnamon
2 tablespoons curry powder
9 garlic cloves, sliced
about 4 tablespoons olive oil
300g (10½oz) couscous
3 tablespoons chopped dried
   apricots
500ml (18fl oz) good-quality
   chicken stock
100g (3½oz) butter, chopped
   into pieces
200g (7oz) cherry tomatoes, halved
100g (3½oz) toasted pine nuts
handful of chopped mint leaves
handful of chopped coriander
salt and black pepper

WE LOVE THIS ONE – IT'S SPECIAL ENOUGH TO LIFT YOUR HEART WHEN IT'S TONIGHT'S SUPPER BUT SIMPLE ENOUGH TO MAKE THAT A REGULAR OCCURRENCE. PLUS IT'S MAINLY MADE WITH STORE CUPBOARD INGREDIENTS SO YOU CAN RUSTLE IT UP IN A HURRY.

Preheat the oven to 220°C (475°F), Gas Mark 9.

Place the chicken pieces in a large baking tray. Mix the chopped preserved lemons, chilli flakes, ground cinnamon, curry powder and half of the sliced garlic with 2 tablespoons of olive oil and toss it in with the chicken. Add the couscous and mix in the apricots. Pour in the stock and dot over the butter, then season well with pepper.

Put the remaining garlic in a bowl, add the tomatoes and drizzle with the remaining oil, enough to coat. Season well with salt and pepper, then scatter the tomatoes over the top of the bake. Cover the tray with foil and bake for 25 minutes, removing the foil after 10 minutes.

To serve, scatter over the pine nuts and herbs and eat immediately.

SPICED KOFTE WITH A QUICK PICKLE SALAD

SERVES 4

HERE YOU GET SUCH A PLEASING MIX: THE HEARTY BASE NOTES OF LAMB AND FLATBREAD WITH THE ZESTY TOP NOTES OF PICKLES AND MINT. WHATEVER COMBINATION IS IN EACH MOUTHFUL, IT'S ALL DELICIOUS.

FOR THE MEATBALLS
750g (1lb 10oz) lamb shoulder, diced
2 small onions, roughly chopped
1 bunch of flat leaf parsley, leaves and stalks finely chopped
1 small bunch of mint, leaves picked and chopped
100g (3½oz) toasted pine nuts, roughly chopped
1½ teaspoons ground cinnamon
1½ teaspoons ground allspice
1 teaspoon black pepper
1 teaspoon salt
olive oil

FOR THE QUICK PICKLE SALAD
1 red onion, finely sliced into half moons
zest and juice of 1 lemon
1 teaspoon red wine vinegar
1 tablespoon pomegranate molasses
1 large cucumber, halved and roughly chopped
2 teaspoons sumac
1 teaspoon nigella seeds
100g (3½oz) pomegranate seeds
1 small bunch of mint, leaves picked

TO SERVE
toasted flatbreads (see page 78 for homemade)
Greek yogurt with a little extra-virgin olive oil and sumac

Put the lamb shoulder and onions in a food processor and pulse until you have a mince-like consistency. Tip into a large bowl along with all the other meatball ingredients apart from the olive oil. With clean hands, squish and mix it all together until well combined. Shape into meatballs roughly the size of golf balls. Cover with a clean tea towel or wax paper and chill in the fridge for 1 hour, or longer if you have time.

About 10 minutes before you want to cook, make the pickle salad. Place the onion in a bowl, add the lemon zest and juice, drizzle over the red wine vinegar and pomegranate molasses, then mix together and set aside for about 5 minutes. After this time, add the cucumber, sumac, nigella and pomegranate seeds, then scatter over the mint leaves and give it a really good mix.

Heat a little oil in a frying pan over a medium heat (you can also do these on a BBQ, if you like). Fry the meatballs until golden brown on all sides, about 20 minutes.

Eat immediately with the quick pickle salad, flatbreads and yogurt.

TIP
IF YOU'RE SHORT ON TIME, YOU COULD USE LAMB MINCE INSTEAD OF LAMB SHOULDER HERE. JUST CHOP THE ONIONS A LITTLE SMALLER IF YOU'RE NOT USING A FOOD PROCESSOR AND THEN COMBINE THE LAMB MINCE AND ONIONS WITH THE REST OF THE MEATBALL INGREDIENTS (EXCEPT FOR THE OLIVE OIL) IN A LARGE BOWL AS ABOVE.

BABAGANOUSH

HAPPILY THE DISH WITH THE BEST NAME IS
ALSO DELICIOUS, SMOKEY AND FLAVOURFUL.

3 aubergines
1 garlic clove, finely chopped
juice of 1 lemon
2 tablespoons tahini
salt and black pepper
extra-virgin olive oil and sumac, to serve

Prick the aubergines a few times, then place directly
on the flames of a gas hob, turning with tongs until
the skins turn black and ashy. If you don't have a gas
hob, simply preheat the grill to full whack and place
them under the grill. When they are black all over,
remove and place in a bowl. Cover the bowl with a
plate and leave until they are cool enough to touch.

Once cool, slice the aubergines in half and use a
spoon to scoop out the flesh onto a large chopping
board, leaving the ashy skin behind.

Add the garlic clove to the aubergine flesh, mashing
it all together. Scoop into a bowl, then squeeze in the
lemon juice. Drizzle in the tahini and mix. Season
with extra-virgin olive oil, salt and pepper and
sumac, to taste.

ZHOUGH

A PERFECT, SPICY, FRESH KICK TO DRIZZLE
OVER MEAT OR STIR THROUGH YOGURT.

3 whole jalapeños, stems removed
2 garlic cloves, peeled
1 bunch of coriander
1 teaspoon ground cumin
1 teaspoon dried Aleppo chilli flakes, or to taste
½ teaspoon ground cardamom
½ teaspoon sea salt flakes, or to taste
1 bunch of mint, leaves picked
200ml (7fl oz) extra-virgin olive oil
juice of ½ lemon

Place all the ingredients, except the oil and lemon
juice, in a food processor and pulse until roughly
chopped. Add the oil and lemon juice and blitz to a
coarse paste. Taste for seasoning and heat, adding
more chilli and salt if you want.

Store in a sealed jar in the fridge for up to a week.

HUMMUS

YOU CAN ADD CORIANDER, PARSLEY OR ANY SOFT HERB FOR A GREEN HUMMUS, BEETROOT
FOR A BRIGHT PINK HUMMUS, OR CHILLI FOR A SPICY VERSION.

660g (1lb 7¼oz) jar of chickpeas
juice of 1 lemon
2 tablespoons tahini
2 tablespoons extra-virgin olive oil, plus extra to serve
½ teaspoon ground cumin
salt, to taste

TO SERVE (OPTIONAL)
toasted pine nuts

Simply tip the chickpeas with the liquid in the jar
into a food processor or blender along with the lemon
juice, tahini, extra-virgin olive oil and ground cumin.
Blend until you have a lovely smooth hummus. Taste,
then season with salt to your taste. Spoon out into a
bowl and top with pine nuts, if using, and a drizzle of
extra-virgin olive oil.

FaLaFeL

THE ONLY WAY TO MAKE GREAT FALAFEL IS TO USE DRIED CHICKPEAS, CANNED WON'T DO. BUT IT'S SO EASY – SIMPLY POUR THEM INTO A BOWL, COVER WITH COLD WATER AND LEAVE OVERNIGHT. THEN JUST DRAIN AND USE.

Drain and rinse the soaked chickpeas and tip them onto a clean tea towel or into a salad spinner to remove any excess water.

Put the chickpeas, along with all the other ingredients except the oil, into a food processor and pulse the mixture until very finely minced, but not puréed, scraping the bowl down as necessary. You should be able to press a handful together and have it hold its shape.

Transfer the falafel mix to a bowl, cover with a plate and chill in the fridge for at least 15 minutes. This will help the balls hold together when cooking. If making ahead, you can refrigerate the mixture for a couple of days.

Scoop out 1 heaped tablespoon of the falafel mix, then gently shape it into a ball and place on a clean plate. Repeat until all the mixture is used up – this should make about 18 balls. (You can chill the balls in the fridge for up to 5 hours if you plan to get ahead.)

Preheat the oven to 160°C (350°F), Gas Mark 4.

Place a large heavy-based casserole dish or saucepan over a medium heat and pour in enough oil to fill the pan by one third. Heat to 180–190°C (350–375°F), or until a cube of bread browns in 30 seconds.

Fry the falafel in batches, lowering them gently into the oil and without crowding the pan, until they are browned on the bottom, then use a slotted spoon to gently flip them to brown on the other side. This should take about 4 minutes in total.

Transfer the cooked falafel to a plate lined with kitchen paper, sprinkle with a little salt, then tip onto a baking tray and place in the oven to keep warm while you repeat with the remaining falafel balls.

Serve on top a generous dollop of Hummus, Babaganoush and Zhough, with the salad leaves and Pink Pickled Onions on the side. Finish with mint leaves, a pinch of sumac and a scattering of pomegranate seeds.

SERVES 4–6

225g (8oz) dried chickpeas, soaked overnight (see introduction)
1 bunch of spring onions, trimmed and halved
4 medium garlic cloves, peeled
1 small bunch of coriander
1 bunch of flat leaf parsley
1 large bunch of mint, leaves picked
3 teaspoons sea salt flakes
2 teaspoons ground cumin
2 teaspoons cumin seeds
1 teaspoon ground coriander
½ teaspoon ground cardamom
½ teaspoon black pepper
¾ teaspoon baking powder
zest of 2 lemons
groundnut oil, for deep-frying

TO SERVE
salt
Hummus (see page 72)
Babaganoush (see page 72)
Zhough (see page 72)
salad leaves
Pink Pickled Onions (see page 146)
mint leaves
pinch of sumac
pomegranate seeds

SMOKED MACKEREL & COUSCOUS SALAD

WHENEVER WE MAKE THIS, WE WONDER WHY WE DON'T MAKE IT MORE OFTEN. FULL OF HEALTH, LIFE AND COLOUR.

SERVES 4

300g (10½oz) giant couscous (or regular couscous if you don't have it)

100g (3½oz) Tenderstem broccoli, separated into florets

½ bunch of flat leaf parsley leaves, chopped

50g (1¾oz) toasted pumpkin seeds

100g (3½oz) pomegranate seeds

150g (5½oz) smoked mackerel fillets (not peppered)

salt

FOR THE SALAD DRESSING

3 tablespoons extra-virgin olive oil

1 red onion, finely chopped

1 teaspoon ground cumin

1 teaspoon honey

finely grated zest and juice of 1 lemon

salt and black pepper, to taste

Fill a medium saucepan half full with water and bring to the boil, add the giant couscous and boil for 6–8 minutes, or until tender. (If using regular couscous, just cover with the boiling water, cover with a lid and leave for 5 minutes.)

Bring a separate saucepan of water to the boil and season with a pinch of salt. Add the broccoli and blanch for 3 minutes, until tender.

Meanwhile, mix the dressing ingredients together in a small bowl, seasoning to taste, and set aside.

When the couscous has had its time, drain well and transfer to a large serving platter.

Drizzle over half of the dressing, add the broccoli and give the couscous a good toss. Scatter over the parsley, pumpkin and pomegranate seeds and finish with flaking the mackerel fillets over the top. Drizzle with the remaining dressing and serve.

QUICK TURKISH FLATBREADS

MAKES 6

MAKING YOUR OWN FLATBREAD IS SO PLEASING AND PRETTY STRAIGHTFORWARD. KEEP IT SIMPLE SERVED WITH JUST BUTTER OR GO FOR ALL THE DIPS AND FILL YOUR BOOTS!

12g (¾oz) fast-action dried yeast
1 teaspoon golden caster sugar
125ml (4fl oz) warm water
180g (6oz) Greek yogurt
1 tablespoon extra-virgin olive oil, plus extra for drizzling
1 heaped teaspoon sea salt flakes
500g (1lb 2oz) plain flour, plus extra for dusting
50g (1¾oz) butter
½ bunch of flat leaf parsley, chopped

TO SERVE (OPTIONAL)
1 teaspoon za'atar
butter, for spreading

Preheat the oven to 160°C (350°F), Gas Mark 4.

Combine the yeast, sugar and measured warm water in a large mixing bowl and stir well. Allow to sit in a warm place for 5–10 minutes, or until the mixture is all bubbly. Whisk in the yogurt, olive oil and salt, then add the flour, butter and chopped parsley and mix with your hands until the dough comes together.

Tip the dough out onto a well-floured work surface and knead for 5 minutes, or until the dough is no longer sticky and springs back when lightly pressed. If the dough is too sticky, you can gradually add a little more flour as you go.

Divide the dough into 6 equal pieces, sprinkle lightly with flour, then cover with a clean tea towel. Allow to rest for 15 minutes.

Place a large frying pan over a medium heat. While the pan is heating, roll out one ball of dough to a rough 20cm (8 inch) circle. Drizzle the top of the dough with a little olive oil and flip it into the pan, oiled-side down. Allow the flatbread to cook for about 1 minute, until the top surface is covered with bubbles and the underside is golden in spots and around the edges. Flip it to the other side and cook for another minute, or until golden spots appear. Slide into the oven to keep warm while you cook the remaining flatbreads.

If you like, you can sprinkle the flatbreads with some za'atar and serve spread with butter.

CHICKEN KEBAB SALAD

SERVES 4

THESE FLAVOURS WORK SO WELL, SO WHY NOT MAKE IT A SALAD? SERVE ON ONE BIG PLATE FOR A COMMUNAL EAT WHICH WILL LOOK SO PRETTY, COLOURFUL AND INVITING.

FOR THE CHICKEN
3 chicken breasts, skinless, chopped into large chunks
150g (5oz) natural yogurt
zest and juice of 1 lemon
1 teaspoon ground cumin
1 teaspoon sweet paprika
1 teaspoon sea salt flakes
1 teaspoon black pepper
1 tablespoon olive oil

FOR THE DRESSING
200g (7oz) natural yogurt
zest and juice of 1 lemon
1 tablespoon tahini
2 garlic cloves, peeled
½ bunch of mint, leaves picked
salt and black pepper

FOR THE PITTA CHIPS
2 pitta breads
3 tablespoons olive oil
1 teaspoon sea salt flakes
1 teaspoon cumin seeds

FOR THE SALAD
½ iceberg lettuce, finely shredded
½ red cabbage, finely shredded
300g (10½oz) vine tomatoes, chopped
1 cucumber, roughly chopped
1 carrot, peeled into thin strips
50g (2oz) pitted black olives
½ bunch of flat leaf parsley, leaves picked
2 tablespoons pomegranate molasses
400g (14oz) can of chickpeas, drained
salt and black pepper

Start with the chicken. This can be done a day in advance and left to marinate, or it can be done and cooked immediately – it's completely up to you. Place all the ingredients for the chicken, apart from the olive oil, in a large mixing bowl. Give it a good mix until well combined, then cover and place in the fridge until you are ready to cook it.

When ready to cook, preheat the oven to 180°C (400°F), Gas Mark 6.

Make the dressing. Simply put all the ingredients in a small blender and blend until smooth. Taste and adjust the seasoning. Set aside.

Place a large frying pan over a medium-high heat. Drizzle in the olive oil and add the chicken. Sear on each side for about 2 minutes or until lovely and golden and slightly catching, then toss every now and again for a further 6 minutes. Once cooked through and golden, remove from the heat and leave to continue cooking slightly in the pan.

Meanwhile, make the pitta chips. Tear the pitta into bite-sized pieces and toss into a large baking tray. Drizzle over the olive oil, season with salt and sprinkle over the cumin seeds. Give it a good toss, making sure all the pittas are evenly coated in oil. Bake for 6 minutes, tossing halfway through, until golden and crisp.

For the salad, arrange the shredded lettuce and cabbage in a large serving platter or bowl, scatter over the tomatoes, cucumber, carrot strips, olives, parsley, pomegranate molasses and chickpeas and toss to combine. Season to taste.

When ready, scatter the pitta chips and chicken over the salad, drizzle with the dressing and serve immediately.

WHOLE HaRISSa-ROaSTeD CaULIFLOWeR
WITH CRISPY ONIONS

SERVES 4

6 garlic cloves, peeled
3 tablespoons rose harissa paste
1 teaspoon sweet paprika
zest and juice of 1 lemon
1 bunch of flat leaf parsley
1 large cauliflower, with
    outer leaves
4 tablespoons dry sherry
400g (14oz) can of chopped
    tomatoes
salt and black pepper

FOR THE CRISPY ONIONS
150ml (5fl oz) vegetable oil
10 shallots, finely sliced
salt

TO SERVE
handful of coriander leaves
handful of mint leaves
pomegranate seeds
flatbreads (optional, see page 78
    for homemade)
Greek yogurt (optional)

ROASTED CAULIFLOWER IS A BIG HIT IN OUR HOME. ROASTING IT WHOLE THIS WAY MEANS YOU GET VERY PLEASING SLICES WHEN YOU DISH UP. THE CAULIFLOWER BECOMES CARAMELISED AND DELICIOUS. EAT AS A MEAL IN ITSELF OR HAVE IT ALONG FOR THE RIDE AS PART OF A FEAST.

Preheat the oven to 180°C (400°F), Gas Mark 6.

Put the garlic in a small blender or food processor along with the harissa, paprika, lemon zest and juice and parsley. Season well with salt and pepper and blitz.

Trim the large outer leaves off the cauliflower, but keep the inner ones on. Trim the base of the cauliflower so it stands on its own. Rub the harissa mixture all over the cauliflower, then place it in a medium casserole dish. Drizzle over the sherry, cover with a lid or foil, and roast for about 30 minutes, or until tender.

Remove from the oven, remove the lid or foil, then pour in the canned tomatoes. Season with salt and pepper and return to the oven for 20 minutes.

Meanwhile, make the crispy onions. Heat the oil in a medium frying pan over a medium heat. Add the shallots to the pan, turn the heat down a little and cook for about 10 minutes until golden and crisp. Move the onions around the pan, making sure they cook evenly. Don't be tempted to turn the heat up. Use a large slotted spoon to scoop the onions out onto a plate lined with kitchen paper, then sprinkle with a little salt and set aside.

Remove the cauliflower from the oven, slice into quarters or thick slices and sprinkle over the herbs, pomegranate seeds and crispy onions. Serve with flatbreads and Greek yogurt, if you like.

PISTACHIO BAKLAVA
WITH ORANGE & HONEY SYRUP

THIS IS SUCH A GORGEOUS PUDDING WHICH WILL FEED A BIG TABLE. IT'S PRETTY EASY TO MAKE BUT TASTES SO INDULGENT AND DELICIOUS. THIS VERSION BRINGS LOVELY LAYERS OF SWEETNESS WITH POMEGRANATE, ORANGE AND HONEY ADDED INTO THE MIX. SERVE WITH A GOOD CUP OF TEA.

MAKES 24 PIECES

100g (3½oz) almonds
200g (7oz) pistachios
2 teaspoons ground cinnamon
½ teaspoon ground cardamom
150g (5½oz) unsalted butter
2 × 270g (9½oz) packets of filo pastry (12 sheets in total)

FOR THE SYRUP
200ml (7fl oz) water
200g (7oz) caster sugar
100ml (3½fl oz) pomegranate juice
100ml (3½fl oz) good-quality runny honey
1 large cinnamon stick
pared zest (3 strips) and juice of 1 orange
finely grated zest of 1 lemon

Preheat the oven to 180°C (400°F), Gas Mark 6 and place a baking sheet on the middle shelf to heat up.

Place all the syrup ingredients in a medium saucepan and bring to a gentle simmer. Let it bubble away, stirring occasionally, for 20 minutes, or until the liquid has reduced by one third. Leave to cool.

Blitz the nuts in a food processor until coarse, then tip into a bowl and stir through the cinnamon and cardamom.

Melt the butter in a small pan, then use a pastry brush to lightly grease a deep, 31 × 28cm (12½ × 11 inch) baking dish with the melted butter.

Unfold the filo pastry sheets and cover with a damp tea towel to stop them from getting dry.

Layer 4 sheets of filo in the base of the baking dish and brush each layer with melted butter. Scatter over half of the nut mixture, then top with another 4 layers of filo, brushing with butter each time. Add the remaining nut mixture, then top with the last 4 layers of filo as before. Generously butter the top. Cut into diamonds with a sharp knife – ensuring the blade goes right to the bottom.

Place on the hot baking sheet and bake for 30–35 minutes, or until golden brown and crisp, reducing the temperature to 170°C (375°F), Gas Mark 5 if the baklava looks as though it is browning too quickly.

Remove the baklava from the oven and spoon half of the cooled syrup over the top. Leave for 5 minutes, then spoon over the remaining syrup. Allow the baklava to cool completely before removing the individual pieces from the dish with a palette knife.

SPICE-FILLED DELIGHTS♥

Spice can take you all the way from a mild smooth korma to all the heat you can handle! Here you can find our family favourites that make sure everyone gets the fire they desire.

CHICKEN STIR-FRY

SALTY AND SWEET, WE LOVE A STIR-FRY. ON YOUR PLATE IN SUPER-QUICK TIME, TOO, SO THE PERFECT MEAL WHEN YOU CRAVE MAXIMUM FLAVOUR IN MINIMUM TIME.

SERVES 4

FOR THE SAUCE
3 tablespoons oyster sauce
2 tablespoons maple syrup, or to taste
2 tablespoons rice wine vinegar
1 tablespoon dark soy sauce, or to taste
1 tablespoon fish sauce
1 tablespoon toasted sesame oil
100ml (3½fl oz) water
zest and juice of 1 lime

FOR THE STIR-FRY
2 tablespoons groundnut oil
100g (3½oz) untoasted cashew nuts
6 chicken thighs, boneless and skinless, chopped into bite-sized pieces
3 garlic cloves, finely sliced
5cm (2 inch) piece of fresh root ginger, peeled and sliced into fine matchsticks
1 bunch of spring onions, trimmed and chopped into 4cm (1½ inch) pieces
2 carrots, pared into thin strips
1 large bunch of Thai basil, leaves only

TO SERVE (OPTIONAL)
jasmine rice
Sichuan-style Chilli Oil (see page 89), if you like spice

For the sauce, simply mix all the ingredients together in a bowl. Taste and adjust the sweetness or saltiness to your liking and set aside.

For the stir-fry, get all your prep done first so you're ready to go. Now is a good time to pop on some rice, if you're serving it with your meal.

Heat 1 tablespoon of the oil in a large frying pan or wok over a medium heat. Toss in the cashew nuts and fry for 4–5 minutes, or until golden all over. Scoop out and set aside.

Increase the heat to high, toss in the chopped chicken and fry for 5 minutes, making sure to move the chicken around the pan so it doesn't catch. Add the remaining tablespoon of oil and chuck in the garlic, ginger and spring onions. Continue to fry for a further minute, tossing everything around to get an even colour. Add the sauce and fry for a further 2 minutes, making sure everything has a good coating. Finally, stir through the fried cashew nuts and carrot strips, rip in the Thai basil leaves and remove from the heat.

Serve immediately with jasmine rice and Sichuan-style Chilli Oil on the side, if you like.

SOME LIKE IT HOT!

AND THAT IS US! BUT AS YOU CAN PROBABLY GUESS, OUR KIDS? NOT SO MUCH. ONE THING THAT WE'VE LEARNT IS THAT WHEN MAKING SPICY FOOD THERE'S NO MIDDLE GROUND. IT TENDS TO BE TOO BLAND FOR SOME, TOO SPICY FOR OTHERS. NOBODY'S HAPPY.

BUT DON'T WORRY, THAT'S WHERE THESE SPICY ADD-INS COME IN. WE ARE MASSIVE HOT SAUCE FANS AND HAVE A COLLECTION FROM TOURING AROUND THE WORLD, BUT THERE'S NOTHING BETTER THAN MAKING YOUR OWN TO ADD SOME FIRE INTO ANY DISH THAT NEEDS IT (TO OUR MIND, ALL DISHES). THESE THREE PRETTY MUCH HAVE YOU COVERED WHETHER GOING FOR INDIAN, FAR EASTERN OR MORE EUROPEAN FLAVOURS AND CAN BE ADDED TO YOUR INDIVIDUAL TASTE. EVERYONE'S A WINNER.

CURRY SPICE ADD-IN

MAKES 1 JAR

FOR CURRIES, SOUPS, STIR THROUGH SCRAMBLED EGGS OR SIMPLY SMEAR OVER BUTTERY PARATHAS FOR A DELICIOUS SNACK.

1 teaspoon whole black peppercorns
4 whole cloves
1 tablespoon yellow mustard seeds
1 tablespoon coriander seeds
2 teaspoons fennel seeds
6 dried red Kashmiri chillies, or any dried red chillies
4 tablespoons ghee or groundnut oil
1 large onion, finely chopped
4 garlic cloves, finely chopped
5cm (2 inch) piece of fresh root ginger, finely chopped
2–4 fresh red chillies (taste and see how hot they are and go by your spice level preference), finely chopped
4 tablespoons tomato purée
1 teaspoon salt
100ml (3½fl oz) water

Place a large dry frying pan over a medium heat, add the peppercorns, cloves, mustard, coriander and fennel seeds and whole dried chillies. Toast for a couple of minutes, tossing the pan until all the spices are toasted and smelling delicious.

Remove the pan from the heat and tip the contents into a food processor, then blitz until you have a rough powder. Set aside.

Put the ghee or oil in the pan and place back over a medium heat. Add the onion, garlic, ginger and fresh chillies and fry for 10 minutes, stirring often so nothing catches. Add the tomato purée and fry for a further 5 minutes, then season with the salt. Tip in the ground spices and measured water and cook over a low heat for a further 10 minutes. If the paste gets too dry, add a little extra water.

Leave the paste to cool, then pour into a sterilised 500ml (18fl oz) jar (it won't fill to the top but it's OK to have a bit of space in the jar) to store in the fridge. Alternatively, freeze in ice-cube trays to pop out whenever you need a spicy curry paste.

SICHUAN-STYLE CHILLI OIL

MAKES 1 JAR

POUR OVER NOODLES, SALADS, FRIED EGGS AND ANYTHING ELSE YOU CAN THINK OF.

500ml (18fl oz) groundnut oil
6 garlic cloves
3 shallots, peeled and halved
5 star anise
1 cinnamon stick
2 dried bay leaves
3 tablespoons Sichuan peppercorns
2 black cardamom pods
2 teaspoons whole cloves
100g (3½oz) Sichuan chilli flakes
5cm (2 inch) piece of fresh root ginger, finely grated
2 teaspoons salt

Pour the oil into a medium saucepan. Bash the garlic and add to the oil – no need to remove the skin. Add the shallots, star anise, cinnamon stick, bay leaves, peppercorns, cardamom pods and cloves. Cook over the very lowest heat for 40 minutes until the garlic and onions are golden and sticky. Meanwhile, combine the Sichuan chilli flakes, ginger and salt in a heatproof bowl.

Remove the pan from the heat, then remove the garlic and shallots from the oil, allow to cool, then finely chop. Add to the bowl.

Check the heat of the oil – it needs to be hot, but not so hot as to burn the chilli flakes. Add a few chilli flakes to the oil in the pan – if they sizzle but don't turn black you are good to go; if they burn, let the oil cool a little. Using a fine sieve, carefully strain the hot oil over the chilli flake mixture. You need to be careful here – it's hot and will sizzle and spit as it hits the chilli flakes. Discard the spices that are left in the sieve and leave the oil to cool.

When cool, pour into a sterilised 1 litre (1¾ pint) glass jar (it won't fill to the top). This will keep in the fridge for up to 3 months, but it won't last that long, I'm sure.

SIMPLE ITALIAN CHILLI OIL

MAKES 1 JAR

FOR PASTAS, PIZZA AND PRETTY MUCH ANYTHING ELSE. ARRABIATA BABY!

handful of chillies (any kind)
10g (¼oz) sea salt flakes
extra-virgin olive oil

Fresh chillies contain a lot of water so first remove the stalks and cut in half. Place them on a plate with kitchen paper and sprinkle with salt. Let them dry out for the next few days occasionally changing the kitchen paper (or you can use dried chillies, of course).

Drop the dried chillies into a sterilised 1 litre (1¾ pint) glass jar (it won't fill to the top but it's OK to have a bit of space in the jar) and top up with the olive oil. Let it rest in a cool, dry place for a day or two and presto!

TIP
TRY ADDING FLAVOURS SUCH AS ROSEMARY, THYME, BAY LEAVES, GARLIC OR PEPPERCORNS. ANYTHING YOU LIKE REALLY!

LEFTOVER LAMB CURRY

THIS CURRY IS SO DELICIOUS MADE WITH LAMB LEFT OVER FROM THE BBQ LAMB ON PAGE 24, BUT HONESTLY IT'S EQUALLY AS GOOD WITHOUT IT. YOU CAN SIMPLY LEAVE OUT THE LAMB AND SERVE AS IS.

Put the fennel and cumin seeds in a small dry frying pan and place over a medium heat. Toast the spices for about 30 seconds or until aromatic, then tip them into a pestle and mortar and grind until you have a rough powder. Set aside.

Place a large heavy-based saucepan over a medium heat. Add the coconut oil, then tip in the mustard seeds and curry leaves and fry until fragrant and the curry leaves are crisp. Add the freshly ground spices and fry for a further 30 seconds. Chuck in the onions, garlic and ginger and fry for 20 minutes, stirring often, until the onions are soft. Add the ground turmeric, red chilli, all the tomatoes and tamarind paste and cook for 10 minutes. Add the coconut milk, pop in the cinnamon stick and leave to cook down and reduce slightly for about 30 minutes, stirring often.

Once the curry has cooked down and is lovely and thick, stir through the leftover lamb. We like to then leave the lamb curry over a low heat for as long as possible to make it nice and tender, but if you're in a rush, you can skip to the next step. About 10 minutes before you're ready to serve, add the spinach to the lamb curry. Cover with a lid, turn off the heat and leave to stand and steam for 10 minutes.

Meanwhile, toast the flaked almonds in a dry frying pan until golden all over.

Season the curry with salt to taste. Remove the chilli and chop it up, to add to dishes for those that like a little heat. Serve with warm parathas or naan breads, a good dollop of yogurt and a sprinkling of coriander leaves.

2 teaspoons fennel seeds
2 teaspoons cumin seeds
2 tablespoons coconut oil
2 teaspoons black mustard seeds
handful of curry leaves
2 onions, finely sliced
4 garlic cloves, peeled and grated
5cm (2 inch) piece of fresh root ginger, peeled and grated
1 teaspoon ground turmeric
1 red chilli
1kg (2lb 4oz) cherry tomatoes on the vine, halved
500g (1lb 2oz) large tomatoes, quartered
1 tablespoon tamarind paste
400g (14oz) can of full-fat coconut milk
1 cinnamon stick
600g (1lb 5oz) leftover cooked lamb (see page 24)
2 handfuls of fresh spinach
salt

TO SERVE
50g (1¾oz) flaked almonds
warm parathas or naan breads
natural yogurt
½ bunch of coriander leaves

KORMA-STYLE PRAWN CURRY

PERFECT FOR THE KIDS. WE SERVE OURS WITH A BIT OF WARM, SPICY PICKLE TO ADD GREAT HEAT FOR THE ADULTS.

SERVES 4

5cm (2 inch) fresh root ginger, chopped
6 garlic cloves, peeled
4 tablespoons Greek yogurt
1 teaspoon mild chilli powder
½ teaspoon ground turmeric
700g (1lb 9oz) jumbo prawns, heads off and deveined
150g (5oz) cashew nuts soaked in boiling water to cover for 20 minutes
3 tablespoons ghee or coconut oil
5 green cardamom pods, bashed
2 black cardamom pods, bashed
4 whole cloves
½ cinnamon stick
3 onions, finely chopped
2 bay leaves
salt

FOR THE PERFECT LEMON RICE
200g (7oz) basmati rice
zest and juice of 1 lemon
½ teaspoon salt
½ teaspoon ground turmeric

QUICK WARM SPICY PICKLE
2 tablespoons ghee or butter
¼ teaspoon each fennel and nigella seeds
½ teaspoon each cumin and black mustard seeds
4 long Indian green chillies, halved lengthways and sliced diagonally
200g (7oz) cherry tomatoes, halved
zest and juice of 1 lime

TO SERVE
almonds, toasted and chopped
handful of coriander leaves
spicy pickle (optional)

Place the ginger and garlic in a small blender with a splash of water and blend to a thick, smooth paste. Transfer to a large bowl along with the yogurt, chilli powder and ground turmeric, season with salt and mix to combine. Toss in the prawns, mix to coat, cover and pop in the fridge until you need them. You can even leave them in the marinade overnight, if you have time. Before cleaning the blender, add the soaked, drained cashew nuts and 5 tablespoons of the soaking liquid, blend to a smooth, creamy paste and set aside.

Melt the ghee or coconut oil in a large, heavy-based saucepan over a medium heat. Add the whole spices, fry for 10 seconds, then add the chopped onions. Reduce the heat to low and cook, stirring frequently, for 20 minutes, until cooked down.

Halfway through cooking the onions, start the lemon rice. Rinse the rice in a colander until the water runs clear, then place in a medium saucepan with a snug-fitting lid. Mix in the lemon zest and juice, salt and turmeric, then add 200ml (7fl oz) cold water. Bring to the boil over a high heat, then reduce the heat right down and cover with the lid. Simmer for 8 minutes, then remove the pan from the heat and leave the lid on for a further 15 minutes.

Meanwhile, add the prawns and their marinade to the onion pan along with the bay leaves and 400ml (14fl oz) cold water, season with salt and simmer over a low heat for 5 minutes, stirring every couple of minutes. Add the cashew paste and simmer for a further 5 minutes, stirring continuously.

Now make the quick pickle. Melt the ghee in a large frying pan, chuck in all the other pickle ingredients and fry for a couple of minutes. Remove and tip into a bowl.

Remove the lid from the rice and fluff with a fork. Serve the curry with the rice on the side, sprinkled with toasted almonds and coriander, and a bowl of the pickle for those who like a little heat.

Pictured overleaf ☞

aubergine CURRY

THIS IS A PERFECT, GENTLE CURRY THAT IS LOVED BY ALL, BUT IF YOU NEED A BIT OF HEAT IN YOUR FOOD, SIMPLY STIR IN A TEASPOONFUL OF OUR CURRY SPICE ADD-IN (SEE PAGE 88).

SERVES 6

FOR THE ROASTED AUBERGINES
5 aubergines (about 700g/1lb 9oz)
1 teaspoon sea salt flakes
1 teaspoon ground turmeric
4 tablespoons ghee or
    coconut oil, melted
juice of 1 lemon

FOR THE SAUCE
2 tablespoons ghee
2 onions, sliced into thin
    half-moons
2 teaspoons black mustard seeds
½ teaspoon ground turmeric
1 tablespoon ground cumin
2 tablespoons ground coriander
2 × 400g (14oz) cans of chopped
    tomatoes
5cm (2 inch) piece of fresh root
    ginger, peeled and grated
5 garlic cloves, peeled and grated
400g (14oz) can of full-fat coconut
    milk
salt

TO SERVE
½ bunch of coriander leaves
chapati or naan breads
rice of your choice (optional)

Preheat the oven to 200°C (425°F), Gas Mark 7.

Remove the woody tops and roughly chop the aubergines into bite-sized chunks, not worrying too much about them all being the same size. Put in a large flat roasting tray and evenly sprinkle with the salt, turmeric and melted ghee or coconut oil. Squeeze the lemon juice over, then use 2 large spoons to toss it all together, making sure everything is evenly coated. Roast for 20 minutes.

Meanwhile, get on with the sauce. Melt the ghee in a large heavy-based pan over a medium heat, add the sliced onions and fry for 10–15 minutes, stirring often, or until soft and translucent. Add the black mustard seeds, ground turmeric, cumin and coriander and fry for a further 3 minutes, stirring all the time. Add the chopped tomatoes and grated ginger and garlic and leave the sauce to reduce and thicken for about 15 minutes.

Remove the aubergines from the oven and give them a good toss. Place back in the oven for a further 10 minutes, checking on them every now and again to make sure they don't burn. Once they are all sticky and slightly charred, remove from the oven.

Tip the roasted aubergines into the sauce pan, and scrape in any bits left on the tray. Pour in the coconut milk, then fill the empty can with water and tip that in too. Reduce the heat to a gentle simmer and cook for a further 25 minutes, stirring occasionally.

Taste the curry and season it with salt to your liking. Remove from the heat and leave to stand for 5 minutes. Serve sprinkled with coriander leaves and with warm naan, chapatis and rice, if you like.

Red Lentil, Squash & Spinach Dhal

SERVES 4–6

1 teaspoon cumin seeds
1 teaspoon coriander seeds
1 teaspoon yellow mustard seeds
2 teaspoons ground turmeric
1 teaspoon garam masala
½ teaspoon dried chilli flakes
1 tablespoon ghee or light olive oil
2 onions, finely sliced
3 garlic cloves, finely chopped
1 tablespoon grated fresh
   root ginger
1 acorn or butternut squash (about
   800g/1lb 12oz), deseeded and
   chopped into small pieces
300g (10½oz) dried red lentils, rinsed
400g (14oz) can of chopped tomatoes
400g (14oz) can of full-fat coconut
   milk
juice of 1 lemon
200g (7oz) baby leaf spinach
salt and black pepper

FOR THE TEMPER
3 tablespoons ghee
3 garlic cloves, finely sliced
handful of curry leaves
2 chillies, sliced
1 teaspoon dried chilli flakes
1 teaspoon black mustard seeds

TO SERVE
poppadoms
good-quality naans or chapati
mango chutney (we love Geeta's)

STIR IN AS MUCH HEAT AS YOU LIKE, BUT, HOT OR MILD, THIS IS A BOWL OF MULTI-LAYERED COMFORT. IT'S ESPECIALLY WARMING WHEN THE NIGHTS ARE DRAWING IN AND THE FIRE IS ROARING.

Toast the cumin, coriander and mustard seeds in a small dry pan over a medium heat for 1–2 minutes until fragrant and starting to pop. Tip into a pestle and mortar and grind until smooth, then add the turmeric, garam masala and dried chilli flakes and mix again. Set aside.

Heat the ghee or oil in a large pan over a medium heat. Add the onions and gently cook for 10–15 minutes until soft and starting to brown. Add the spice mix, garlic and ginger and cook for a few minutes, then add the squash and continue to fry for a further 10 minutes. Add the lentils, chopped tomatoes and coconut milk, then fill the empty coconut milk can with cold water twice and add both canfuls to the pan too. Season with salt and pepper and simmer over a medium heat for 20 minutes, stirring occasionally.

Add the lemon juice and spinach to the pan and cover with a lid to let the spinach wilt.

Meanwhile, make the temper. Place a small pan over a high heat, add the ghee followed by the garlic and fry until the garlic starts to turn golden. Add the curry leaves and sliced chillies and fry for a further minute, then add the chilli flakes and mustard seeds and fry for 30 seconds. Remove from the heat and pour into a bowl.

Ladle the dhal into bowls and top with a spoonful of the temper for those who like spice. Serve with poppadoms, warmed naan breads or chapati and mango chutney. Leave the bowl of temper on the table to add as you go.

Pictured overleaf ☞

CRISPY paneer salad

MIGHT HAVE MENTIONED THIS BEFORE BUT... WE LOVE A SALAD. THIS ONE IS SUPER HEARTY. GHEE MAKES THE FLAVOUR ALL THE MORE AUTHENTIC.

SERVES 4

FOR THE CRISPY PANEER
2 tablespoons ghee
250g (9oz) paneer, cut into 3cm (1¼ inch) cubes
1 teaspoon black mustard seeds

FOR THE SALAD
1 red onion, finely chopped
4 mixed carrots, peeled into long strips
200g (7oz) spinach, roughly torn
400g (14oz) can of chickpeas, drained and rinsed
100g (3½oz) pomegranate seeds
1 bunch of coriander leaves
100g (3½oz) Bombay mix

FOR THE DRESSING
100ml (3½fl oz) natural yogurt
½ teaspoon garam masala
½ bunch of coriander, finely chopped
½ green chilli, finely chopped
1 teaspoon water

TO SERVE
1 tablespoon tamarind sauce

To make the crispy paneer, melt the ghee in a medium frying pan over a medium heat. Add the paneer and fry on one side until golden, then turn and continue to fry until golden on all sides. Add the mustard seeds for the last minute of frying.

Meanwhile, mix all the salad ingredients together on a large platter.

Mix together all the dressing ingredients.

Toss the salad together with the crispy paneer and drizzle over the dressing, finishing with drizzles of the tamarind sauce. Serve immediately.

LYCHEE & LEMONGRASS GRANITA

SERVES 4–6

YOU CAN TOP THIS WITH PROSECCO, TOO, FOR A BOOZY ADULT PUDDING.

10 lemongrass stalks
1 vanilla pod, split lengthways
150g (5½oz) granulated sugar
400g (14oz) can of lychees in syrup, drained, reserving the syrup
1 litre (1¾ pints) cold water
zest and juice of 4 limes, plus extra zest to serve

Cut the lemongrass stalks in half lengthways and bash roughly with the back of the knife or a rolling pin. Place in a medium heavy-based pan with the split vanilla pod, the sugar and the syrup from the lychees. Pour in the measured water and bring to the boil over a medium heat. Remove from the heat and leave the syrup to cool completely.

Tip the drained lychees into a blender and blitz until smooth. Add the lime zest and juice and blitz until incorporated.

Once the syrup has cooled, pour in the lychee mixture and mix it in well. Pour the mixture into a lidded airtight container (about 25 × 15 × 4cm/10 × 6 × 1½ inches). Cover with the lid and place in the freezer.

After 2 hours, check on the granita. It should have started to freeze around the edges and on the base. Using a fork, mix the ice crystals back into the mixture and return it to the freezer. Repeat this process every hour for a further 5–6 hours, or until you have a lovely crystalline iced mixture.

If left overnight, the granita will freeze solid, so allow it to soften in the fridge for 30 minutes and remix with a fork before serving, sprinkled with the extra lime zest.

FAR EAST INSPIRED♥

Of all the flavours around the world, we think these are the ones we'd pick if we were only to eat one group for the rest of our lives. Endlessly delicious and evocative, these dishes are adored by the whole family from top to bottom and are the most often requested for birthday meals by our kids, too!

BUILD-YOUR-OWN SUSHI TACOS

THIS IS REALLY EASY AND ENJOYABLE FOR THE WHOLE FAMILY TO MAKE. ALL THE WONDERFUL FLAVOURS OF SUSHI BUT WITHOUT THE FUSS. IT'S A LITTLE MESSY, WHICH ADDS TO THE FUN.

150g (5½oz) – or 1 cup – sushi rice

300ml (11fl oz) – or 2 cups – water

2 tablespoons sushi rice seasoning (Mizkan Sushizu Vinegar is our fave brand, or make your own by stirring together 1½ tablespoons rice vinegar and 1 teaspoon caster sugar)

TO SERVE

3 nori sheets

1 avocado

½ cucumber

100g (3½oz) sushi-grade salmon or tuna fillet, skinned, or 60g (2¼oz) store-bought crab sticks

50g (1¾oz) store-bought crispy onions

toasted sesame seeds, for sprinkling (see Tip)

soy sauce, for dipping

wasabi (optional)

pickled ginger (optional)

MAKES 12

Put the rice and water in a medium saucepan. We like to use a cup as it's quick and easy, simply use the same cup to measure double the volume of water – we find this is the perfect amount. Bring to the boil, then cover and cook over a medium heat for 12–14 minutes. If you can, use a glass lidded saucepan, so you can see when all the water has been absorbed. Remove from the heat and leave the lid on for a further 15 minutes.

Season the rice with the sushi rice seasoning, then taste and adjust to your liking. Transfer the rice to a large, shallow tray (this helps cool the rice as quickly as possible). Set aside, covered with a damp cloth, to cool completely while you prepare the nori and other fillings.

Cut each nori sheet into 4 rounds, each about 10cm (4 inches) in diameter. (Round tacos look pretty but we also find rectangles easier for very little hands.) Place on a plate, these will be your taco shells. Stone, skin and quarter the avocado, then cut into thin slices. Slice the cucumber into sticks. Cut the salmon or tuna into 6cm (2½ inch) pieces or roughly shred the crab sticks. Put all the fillings into separate bowls.

To serve, let the kids build their own sushi tacos, with soy sauce for dipping and wasabi and pickled ginger for those that like it.

TIP

YOU CAN MAKE YOUR OWN TOASTED SESAME
SEEDS BY TOASTING SESAME SEEDS IN A DRY
FRYING PAN FOR A FEW MINUTES, BUT WE
BUY THEM READY-TOASTED AND READY TO
SPRINKLE FROM OUR LOCAL ASIAN FOOD
STORE. THEY COME IN BOTH WHITE
AND BLACK VARIETIES.

CHIRASHI BOWL

SERVES 2

THIS CHIRASHI BOWL IS QUICK AND EASY, AND SOMETHING WE OFTEN MAKE WHEN THE KIDS ARE HAVING THE BUILD-YOUR-OWN SUSHI TACOS (SEE PAGE 108), AS IT'S ESSENTIALLY ALL THE SAME INGREDIENTS. IF YOU CAN'T GET REALLY FRESH FISH, WHICH HAPPENS TO US SOMETIMES, OR YOU DON'T LIKE RAW FISH, WE DO THE SAME RECIPE BUT JUST COOK THE FISH IN A LITTLE TERIYAKI SAUCE, WHICH IS EQUALLY DELICIOUS.

150g (5½oz) – or 1 cup – sushi rice
300ml (10fl oz) – or 2 cups – water
2 tablespoons sushi rice seasoning
   (Mizkan is our fave brand or
   make your own, see page 108)

OPTIONAL TOPPINGS (YOU REALLY CAN MAKE THIS UP BUT HERE'S THE STUFF WE LIKE)
sushi-grade salmon or tuna,
   roughly chopped
salmon/red flying fish roe
edamame beans
toasted sesame seeds
chopped chives
pomegranate seeds
avocado, roughly chopped
crab sticks, roughly shredded
cucumber, chopped into sticks
nori sheets, chopped or finely
   chopped as a sprinkle (these can
   also be used whole to scoop up
   from the bowl and eat directly)

TO SERVE
soy sauce
Japanese Kewpie mayonaise
sriracha sauce (for the grown ups)

Put the rice and water in a medium saucepan. We like to use a cup as it's quick and easy, simply use the same cup to measure double the volume of water – we find this is the perfect amount. Bring to the boil, then cover and cook over a medium heat for 12–14 minutes. If you can, use a glass lidded saucepan, so you can see when all the water has been absorbed. Remove from the heat and leave the lid on for a further 15 minutes.

Season the rice with the rice seasoning, then taste and adjust to your liking. Allow to cool slightly before serving.

Divide the rice between 2 bowls and add all the toppings of your choice. Finish with a little soy sauce drizzled over the top or served in a separate small bowl for dipping, with the Kewpie mayonnaise and sriracha sauce for those who like it hot.

KIDS LOVE MAKI

DON'T BE AFRAID TO MAKE YOUR OWN! IT'S SO MUCH FUN. ALTHOUGH WE ALWAYS HAVE TO MAKE ABOUT DOUBLE AS OUR KIDS EAT A *LOT* OF MAKI. SERIOUSLY, TONS. THIS RECIPE IS FOR THEIR FAVOURITE SALMON AND AVOCADO INSIDE-OUT ROLLS, BUT DON'T BE SCARED TO TRY OTHER COMBINATIONS. ALSO, OURS OFTEN COME OUT A LITTLE WONKY BUT YOU'RE NOT CHASING PERFECTION HERE – IT'S ALL ABOUT TASTE.

SERVES 6 (MAKES 36 ROLLS)

100g (3½oz) – or 1 cup – sushi rice
200ml (7fl oz) – or 2 cups – water
2 tablespoons sushi rice seasoning
    (see page 108 to make your own)
2 avocados
150g (5½oz) sushi-grade skinless
    salmon, or crab sticks
6 nori sheets
3 tablespoons mixed sesame seeds

FOR THE SPICY SRIRACHA MAYO
3 tablespoons mayonnaise
1 tablespoon sriracha sauce
juice of ½ lime
salt and black pepper

FOR THE SWEET SOY SAUCE
2 tablespoons soy sauce
1 tablespoon rice vinegar
1 tablespoon runny honey
1 teaspoon toasted sesame oil

Put the rice and water in a medium saucepan. We like to use a cup as it's quick and easy, simply use the same cup to measure double the volume of water – we find this is the perfect amount. Bring to the boil, then cover and cook over a medium heat for 12–14 minutes. If you can, use a glass lidded saucepan, so you can see when all the water has been absorbed. Remove from the heat and leave the lid on for a further 15 minutes.

Season the rice with the rice seasoning, then taste and adjust to your liking. Transfer the rice to a large, shallow tray (this helps cool the rice as quickly as possible). Set aside, covered with a damp cloth, to cool completely while you prepare the fillings.

Stone, skin and quarter the avocados, then cut into long thin strips. If using salmon, thinly slice into long strips.

To assemble the rolls, lay a nori sheet on a board. (We cut a quarter off the top of ours so the rolls don't end up too big, and then we can use the cut part for sushi tacos.) Spread one-sixth of the rice over two-thirds of the nori sheet. Lay a sheet of clingfilm over a sushi rolling mat and sprinkle with sesame seeds. Flip the nori and rice onto the mat, rice-side down, with the empty space at the top. We get the kids to help with this – it makes a bit of mess, but is lots of fun!

Line slices of avocado and salmon or crab sticks across the middle of the nori sheet to create the filling. Use the mat to roll it all up into a log to enclose the filling, rolling from the edge nearest you towards the top of the nori sheet with no rice on it. Remove the clingfilm and trim away the excess nori.

Repeat with the remaining ingredients to make 6 logs. Cut each log into 6 equal pieces to give 36 rolls in total. When cutting, I think it's really helpful to have a damp cloth nearby (I put the cloth in a little bowl of water, so I can also use it to clean sticky fingers), to wipe the knife every so often in-between cuts. It slices through the rice much more cleanly and easily this way.

To make the spicy sriracha mayo, simply mix together all the ingredients in a small bowl and taste for seasoning. Similarly, to make the sweet soy sauce, mix the ingredients together in a small bowl (it's unlikely to need any further seasoning due to the soy sauce).

Serve the rolls with the spicy sriracha mayo and sweet soy sauce on the side for dipping.

SMASHING CUCUMBER SALAD

SERVES 4 AS A SIDE

THIS IS PERFECT ALONGSIDE KIMCHI FRIED RICE (SEE PAGE 118) OR THE POACHED CHICKEN & RICE SOUP (SEE PAGE 120).

2 large cucumbers
1 garlic clove, peeled
2.5cm (1 inch) piece of fresh root
   ginger, peeled
½ bunch of coriander, chopped
1 tablespoon soy sauce
1 teaspoon toasted sesame oil
2 tablespoons rice wine vinegar
1 teaspoon caster sugar
3 tablespoons toasted sesame seeds
Sichuan-style Chilli Oil (see
   page 89), to serve (optional)

Slice the cucumbers in half lengthways. Using a spoon, bash the cucumber skin all over, then chop into 3cm (1¼ inch) slices diagonally. Transfer to a mixing bowl. Grate in the garlic and ginger and stir in the chopped coriander. Pour over the soy sauce, sesame oil, rice wine vinegar and sugar and toss it all together. Toss in the sesame seeds and adjust the seasoning to your liking, adding a drizzle of Sichuan-style Chilli Oil, if you like.

CRISPY HAM, PEAR & TUNA SALAD

THIS IS OUR VERSION OF A SALAD WE TRIED ONCE ON HOLIDAY AND FELL IN LOVE WITH. THE COMBINATION OF FLAVOURS IS SO GOOD. DID I MENTION WE LOVE A SALAD?

SERVES 4

2 tablespoons olive oil
8 prosciutto slices
100g (3½oz) edamame beans
2 ripe pears
500g (1lb 2oz) mixed tomatoes
1 cucumber
4 tablespoons black sesame seeds
3 × 100g (3½oz) tuna steaks
1 bunch of coriander leaves
salt
Sichuan-style Chilli Oil (see
    page 89), to serve (optional)

FOR THE DRESSING
2 tablespoons sushi rice seasoning
1 tablespoon soy sauce, or to taste
zest and juice of 1 lime
5cm (2 inch) piece of fresh root
    ginger, grated

Heat 1 tablespoon of the oil in a large pan over a high heat, add the prosciutto and fry for about 3 minutes on each side, or until crisp and golden. Remove the prosciutto from the pan and set aside on a plate. Remove the pan from the heat, but keep it handy as you'll use it again.

Mix all the ingredients for the dressing in a bowl. Taste and add a little extra soy sauce, if needed.

Bring a small saucepan of water to the boil over a high heat. Add the edamame beans and boil for 2 minutes, or until vivid green but still with a little bite. Drain and set aside.

Slice the pears in half and chop out the cores, then roughly slice. Slice the larger tomatoes and quarter the smaller ones. Shave the cucumber into ribbons with a vegetable peeler. Toss it all onto a big serving platter along with the cooked edamame. Sprinkle over a little salt and half of the dressing and toss to combine.

Place the pan back over a high heat. Tip the sesame seeds onto a plate and roll the tuna steaks in the seeds, ensuring they are evenly coated.

Drizzle the remaining tablespoon of oil into the frying pan and gently place the tuna in. Fry for 1½ minutes on each side, then remove from the pan and leave to cool a little.

Slice the tuna up and place on top of the salad platter. Crumble the prosciutto over the top and scatter over the coriander leaves. Drizzle over a little more dressing and serve the rest on the side. This is also great with a drizzle of our Sichuan-style Chilli Oil.

Pictured overleaf

KIMCHI FRIED RICE

SERVES 4

4 tablespoons groundnut oil

2 chicken breasts, chopped into
  bite-sized pieces

2 garlic cloves, peeled and grated

5cm (2 inch) piece of fresh root ginger,
  peeled and grated

4 tablespoons teriyaki sauce

200g (7oz) green beans, roughly
  chopped

300g (10½ oz) sushi rice, cooked and
  cooled (see page 108) or leftover

450g (1lb) jar of kimchi (we use Biona),
  roughly chopped

2 tablespoons gochujang

2 large free-range eggs

TO SERVE
handful of coriander leaves
3 spring onions, chopped
2 tablespoons toasted sesame seeds
juice of 1 lime
Sichuan-style Chilli Oil (see page 89)
  or sriracha (optional)

OOH, THIS IS A GOOD ONE. EVERY MOUTHFUL IS PACKED WITH FLAVOUR AND HEAT – A BOWL OF FUN WHERE YOU CAN PLAY WITH THE INGREDIENTS AND MAKE IT YOUR OWN. WHENEVER WE EAT THIS, IT REMINDS US OF A BRILLIANT TRIP TO SEOUL WHERE WE ATE BIBIMBAP DAILY.

Place a large pan or wok over a high heat. Add half the oil to the hot pan, then toss in the chicken and fry for about 2 minutes on each side until golden brown. Add the garlic and ginger and fry for 1 minute, then pour in the teriyaki sauce and cook for a further minute, or until sticky and reduced a little. Scoop the mixture out of the pan into a bowl.

Add the remaining oil to the pan and heat for a minute. Add the green beans and fry for a minute, then add the cooked sushi rice. Toss the rice about the pan, then leave untouched for 5 minutes to get crispy. Add the kimchi and gochujang and fry for another 5 minutes, stirring it all together. Return the chicken mixture to the pan and stir to combine. Crack in the eggs and fry for a further minute, stirring a little to break up the eggs slightly, then remove from the heat.

Ladle into bowls, top each with a sprinkle of coriander leaves, spring onions, toasted sesame seeds and a squeeze of lime juice and eat immediately. This is also good with a drizzle of our Sichuan-style Chilli Oil or sriracha, if you like more spice.

POACHED CHICKEN & RICE SOUP WITH CUCUMBER SALAD & SWEET SOY DIPPING SAUCE

THIS IS SUCH A WINNER WITH THE JONES CLAN. IT'S THAT RARE THING: A MEAL THAT GETS THE THUMBS UP FROM EVERYONE! FOR VEGGIE RAY WE USE VEGETABLE STOCK AND SUBSTITUTE CHICKEN FOR TOFU, WHICH IS ALSO REALLY TASTY.

SERVES 4

FOR THE SOUP
5 garlic cloves, smashed with the back of a knife
5cm (2 inch) piece of fresh root ginger, sliced
½ bunch of spring onions, sliced
4 whole star anise
2 litres (3½ pints) good-quality chicken stock
2.5kg (5lb 8oz) whole chicken
200g (7oz) basmati or jasmine rice
a few coriander sprigs, chopped

FOR THE DIPPING SAUCE
2.5cm (1 inch) piece of fresh root ginger
1 garlic clove
½ bunch of spring onions, finely sliced
100ml (3½fl oz) tamari or light soy sauce
2 tablespoons toasted sesame oil
1 tablespoon brown sugar
1 tablespoon hoisin sauce
a few coriander sprigs, chopped
salt and black pepper

FOR THE SALAD
1 cucumber, chopped
drizzle of soy sauce
drizzle of toasted sesame oil

Start with poaching the chicken. Place the garlic, ginger, spring onions and star anise in a heavy-based saucepan that has a lid and pour in the stock. Place the whole chicken in the pan, breast-side up. Bring to a rolling boil, then reduce the heat to a gentle simmer. Place a lid on the pan and leave to simmer for 1 hour.

Carefully remove the poached chicken from the stock and leave to rest covered with a tea towel. Strain the stock through a fine-mesh sieve into a clean saucepan and place back over a low heat.

Place the rice in a medium saucepan that has a snug-fitting lid. Measure out 500ml (18fl oz) of the hot stock and pour over the rice, then bring to the boil. Place the lid on the pan, reduce the heat to low and cook for 10 minutes. Remove from the heat and leave to stand with the lid on for a further 5 minutes.

To make the dipping sauce, simply grate the ginger and garlic into a medium bowl and mix in all the remaining ingredients with 1 tablespoon of the chicken stock until well combined. Taste and adjust the seasoning.

For the cucumber salad, place the cucumber in a bowl. Season with a little soy sauce and a drizzle of sesame oil and place on the table with the bowl of dipping sauce.

Slice the chicken breast into strips widthways, and shred the meat from the legs.

Remove the lid from the rice and give it a good fluff
with a fork, then scoop the rice into 4 bowls. Ladle a
little hot chicken stock into each bowl, top with the
chicken and a sprinkle of coriander leaves.

Serve immediately with the salad and dipping sauce.
Dip and slurp away.

Pictured overleaf ☞

OUR CHICKEN NOODLE SOUP

THIS ALSO WORKS AS A REALLY EASY LUNCH IF YOU JUST USE GOOD-QUALITY FRESH STOCK FROM THE SUPERMARKET, POACHING THE CHICKEN BREASTS IN IT AS BELOW.

FOR THE STOCK
10cm (4 inch) piece of fresh root
   ginger, roughly sliced
   not peeled
2 lemongrass stalks, bashed
1 cinnamon stick
6 star anise
3 litres (5¼ pints) chicken stock
2 tablespoons fish sauce,
   or to taste
600g (1lb 5oz) thick pho rice
   noodles
4–6 chicken breasts
1 tablespoon toasted sesame oil
3 tablespoons white miso paste,
   or to taste
juice of 2 limes

TO SERVE
1 bunch of mint, leaves picked
1 bunch of Thai basil, leaves
   picked
4 spring onions, sliced
   diagonally
1 onion, finely sliced
300g (10½oz) fresh beansprouts
2 fresh red chillies, sliced
hot chilli sauce, such as
   sriracha, or Sichuan-style
   Chilli Oil (see page 89)

Chuck the ginger, lemongrass, cinnamon stick and star anise into your largest saucepan, set over a high heat and toast until fragrant, about 3 minutes. Pour in the stock and fish sauce and leave to simmer.

While the stock is bubbling away, cook the rice noodles according to the packet instructions and plunge into cold water until you need them.

Add the chicken breasts to the stock and poach in the liquid for 10 minutes.

Meanwhile, prepare your serving accompaniments and pile on a board or platter.

Remove the poached chicken breasts from the stock, place on a plate and drizzle over the sesame oil. Leave to cool a little. Add the miso paste and lime juice to the stock and give it a good whisk. Taste and add a little extra miso or fish sauce, if you like.

Divide the noodles between 4–6 bowls, slice the chicken breasts, making sure the chicken is cooked through, and divide among the bowls.

Strain the stock through a fine-mesh sieve into a clean pan and discard the spices and ginger. Ladle the stock into the noodle bowls, then let everyone build their own bowl with the serving accompaniments. Ideally, top with mint, Thai basil, spring onions, sliced onion, beansprouts and chopped chilli, then finish with a drizzle of Sichuan-style Chilli Oil or sriracha and slurp away.

CRISPY TOFU & peanut noodles

WHO DOESN'T LOVE NOODLES? QUICK, TASTY AND VERSATILE, THIS RECIPE IS A GREAT SPEEDY OPTION THAT USES MAINLY STORE CUPBOARD INGREDIENTS. FEEL FREE TO RAMP UP THE HEAT WITH CHILLI OIL, YOU KNOW HOW HOT YOU LIKE IT!

SERVES 4

2 tablespoons groundnut oil
280g (10oz) extra-firm tofu,
    chopped into 2cm (¾ inch) cubes
350g (12oz) dried egg noodles
3 tablespoons sesame seeds
2 carrots
100g (3½oz) beansprouts
1 small bunch of spring onions,
    finely sliced
1 large bunch of coriander,
    leaves picked
Sichuan-style Chilli Oil (see
    page 89), to serve (optional)

FOR THE SAUCE
2 garlic cloves
1cm (½ inch) piece of fresh
    root ginger
5 tablespoons crunchy peanut
    butter
2 tablespoons toasted sesame oil
2 tablespoons groundnut oil
3 tablespoons rice wine vinegar

To make the sauce, grate the garlic and ginger into a mixing bowl, add the remaining ingredients and whisk until smooth.

Heat the groundnut oil in a large frying pan over a high heat, add the tofu and fry on each side until golden and crisp, roughly 2 minutes on each side.

Meanwhile, bring a medium saucepan of water to the boil, then add the noodles and cook for 3 minutes or until a little al dente. Drain and place in a serving bowl.

Once the tofu is golden and crisp all over, toss in the sesame seeds and toast for a minute, then remove from the heat.

Use a julienne peeler or vegetable peeler to pare strips of the carrot into the noodle bowl, then add the beansprouts and the sauce and toss to combine. Top with the tofu, spring onions and coriander. Finish with some Sichuan-style Chilli Oil, if you like it hot.

coconut & lime easy peasy panna cotta

THESE CAN BE MADE UP TO TWO DAYS IN ADVANCE – JUST MAKE THE TOASTED COCONUT TOPPING ON THE DAY YOU SERVE IT SO IT'S NICE AND CRISP. IF YOU DON'T HAVE MOULDS, SIMPLY SET THESE IN TEACUPS OR BOWLS AND DON'T TURN THEM OUT.

SERVES 4

6 gelatine leaves
400ml (14fl oz) double cream
2 × 400g (14oz) cans of full-fat
    coconut milk
100g (3½oz) golden caster sugar
1 teaspoon vanilla bean paste
zest of 4 limes (reserve the juice for the
    topping and a little zest to serve)

FOR THE TOPPING
100g (3½oz) coconut flakes
1 tablespoon maple syrup
1 mango, sliced

Place the gelatine leaves in a small bowl and cover in cold water. Leave for 5 minutes to soften.

Place the double cream, coconut milk, sugar, vanilla bean paste and lime zest in a medium heavy-based saucepan. Pop over a medium heat and stir until the sugar is dissolved. Bring to the boil, add the softened gelatine leaves, then remove from the heat.

Strain the liquid through a fine-mesh sieve into a jug, then pour the mixture into 6 canelé moulds (or see recipe introduction). Refrigerate for 6 hours or until set.

To make the topping, put the coconut flakes in a large dry frying pan set over a medium heat. Toss the coconut around until it turns golden. Remove from the heat and stir in the maple syrup.

To turn the panna cottas out, boil a kettle and fill a heatproof bowl with boiling water. Run a knife around the edge of the moulds, then dunk the bottom of the moulds in the water for 3 seconds. Turn the puddings out onto a small plate and top with the mango, the reserved lime juice and zest, and toasted coconut.

Mexican Fiesta♥ Tribute

We've been lucky enough to go to Mexico for business and pleasure and it's one of our favourite places on earth. Brimming with vitality, colour and excitement at every turn, the food is a joy to behold and perfect for feasts with friends. That is why we have it for our joint birthday celebrations every year!

MEXICAN BRUNCH

THIS CAN BE ADAPTED TO EVERYONE'S TASTE: TRY BLACK
BEANS INSTEAD OF CHORIZO, OR TOP WITH CHEDDAR IF YOU
DON'T LIKE FETA. YOU CAN EVEN SERVE ALL THE TOPPINGS
ON THE SIDE AND EVERYONE CAN ADD WHAT THEY LIKE.
PLUS THIS MAKES THE PERFECT BRUNCH FOR THE MORNING
AFTER THE NIGHT BEFORE.

SERVES 4

2–3 tablespoons olive oil
4 flour tortillas
300g (10½oz) cooking chorizo,
    roughly chopped
500g (1lb 2oz) fresh vine tomatoes,
    sliced
1 teaspoon sweet paprika
juice of 2 limes
1 corn on the cob
1 avocado, halved, stoned and flesh
    roughly sliced
8 free-range eggs
large knob of butter
1 small bunch of coriander, leaves
    picked
200g (7oz) feta cheese, crumbled
salt and black pepper

TO SERVE (OPTIONAL)
pickled jalapeño peppers
Mexican hot sauce
Pink Pickled Onions (see page 146)

Preheat the oven to 100°C (250°F), Gas Mark ½.

Heat 1 tablespoon of the oil in a large frying pan over a high heat. Add
each tortilla one at a time and fry for 1–2 minutes on each side until
crispy and golden all over. Remove and pop in the oven on a large baking
tray to keep warm. Continue until all the tortillas are cooked.

Add the chorizo to the pan with no extra oil and fry for about 6 minutes
until golden and crispy. Use a slotted spoon to scoop the chorizo into a
bowl, leaving any excess oil behind.

Add the tomato slices to the pan, with a little extra oil if you need it. Place
over a high heat and fry until charred, then flip and cook on the other
side. Don't worry if the tomatoes start to break down a little. Sprinkle in
the paprika, the juice of 1 lime and plenty of salt and pepper. Leave over a
very low heat while you prepare the remaining ingredients.

Shave the corn kernels from the cob with a sharp knife into a medium
bowl. Place the avocado in a separate bowl and squeeze the juice of the
second lime over the top. Crack the eggs into a third bowl and whisk.

Heat 1 tablespoon of olive oil and the butter in another frying pan over
a medium heat. Add the eggs to the pan and quickly scramble, making
sure not to overcook them.

Remove the tortillas from the oven and place one on each plate. Spread
over the tomatoes and top each with a spoonful of scrambled eggs.
Scatter over the raw corn, avo and crispy chorizo, then finish with a
scattering of coriander leaves and a crumbling of feta.

If you like, serve with pickled jalapeños and Mexican hot sauce for extra
heat or with some Pink Pickled Onions for an extra kick.

sea bass ceviche

SUPER ZINGY AND DELICIOUS. WHENEVER WE MAKE THIS, WE EAT IT UNTIL THE PLATES ARE SQUEAKY CLEAN. IT'S SUCH AN EXCITING MIX OF FLAVOURS – FULL OF VITALITY AND ZEST.

SERVES 2

**2 sea bass fillets, skinned, sliced
    into 3cm (1¼ inch) chunks**
2 limes
**½ bunch of coriander: stalks finely
    chopped, leaves picked**
1 extra-large ripe avocado
8 radishes, finely sliced
1 small red onion, finely chopped
1 large ripe tomato, roughly chopped
1 fresh jalapeño chilli, sliced
olive oil, for drizzling
salt and black pepper
**purple or regular corn tortilla chips,
    to serve**

Place the sea bass chunks in a glass or ceramic bowl. Grate in the zest of 1 lime, then squeeze in the juice of both limes. Season well with salt and pepper and stir through the chopped coriander stalks. Place in the fridge for 20 minutes.

Meanwhile, slice the avocado in half and remove the stone, scoop out the flesh and finely slice.

Once the fish has had its time, remove and toss all the ingredients, except the oil and tortilla chips, together in a large bowl. Divide between 2 plates, scatter over the coriander leaves and drizzle with a little olive oil.

Serve with plenty of tortilla chips to scoop it up.

CHICKEN FAJITAS

THIS IS A STAPLE PART OF OUR FOOD ROSTER, EVERYONE LOVES IT. YOU CAN'T GO WRONG WITH CHICKEN FAJITAS (AND THE VEGETARIAN JUST HAS HIS WITHOUT THE CHICKEN).

SERVES 4

FOR THE FAJITA SPICE MIX
1 tablespoon ground cumin
1 tablespoon cracked black pepper
1 tablespoon ground coriander
1 tablespoon sweet smoked paprika
1 tablespoon dried oregano
1 teaspoon chilli powder
1 teaspoon sea salt flakes
1 tablespoon soft brown sugar

FOR THE FAJITAS
4 mixed peppers, deseeded and sliced into
    3cm (1¼ inch) strips
2 red onions, each chopped into 8 wedges
4 garlic cloves, smashed
2 red chillies
2 tablespoons olive oil
4 skinless boneless chicken breasts, sliced
    into 3cm (1¼ inch) strips
1 teaspoon cumin seeds
juice of 2 limes

TO SERVE
8 flour tortillas, warmed

OPTIONAL
shredded lettuce
soured cream
grated Cheddar cheese
Our Guacamole (see page 146)
Pink Pickled Onions (see page 146)
Tomato Salsa (see page 147)
Mexican hot sauce

If you are making your own guacamole, pickled onions and salsa (very popular in our house), make those bits first and set them aside.

Next, the spice mix. Simply mix all the ingredients together in a clean airtight container (see Tip) and set aside. This will keep for up to 2 months as long as it's well sealed.

Place your largest frying pan over a high heat. Chuck the pepper strips into the hot dry pan along with the onions, garlic and the whole chillies. Toss the pan and leave everything to char for about 6 minutes, tossing every now and again.

Remove the chillies from the pan and slice up into a bowl for those who like them.

Pour the olive oil into the pan and add the chicken strips. Toss it all together, then add 2 tablespoons of the spice mix and fry for 3 minutes. Sprinkle in the cumin seeds, squeeze in the lime juice and continue to fry for a further 3 minutes. Remove from the heat and tip into a bowl.

Serve with warmed tortillas and any other bits you like.

TIP
WE MAKE LOTS OF THIS SPICE MIX AND KEEP IT IN AN AIRTIGHT CONTAINER FOR SPEEDY DINNERS: SCALE UP IN THE SAME PROPORTIONS.

Pictured overleaf ☞

OUR CHILLI BOWL

WHEN YOU HAVE TO SERVE LOTS OF PEOPLE WITH DIFFERENT FOOD PREFERENCES, THIS IS A WAY TO MAKE ONE MEAL WITH CUSTOMISED TOPPINGS THAT WILL SUIT ALL. THIS IMPROVES WITH TIME, SO IF YOU MAKE IT THE DAY BEFORE EATING IT'LL BE EVEN BETTER. WE SERVE IT WITH RICE BUT YOU COULD ALSO SERVE IT WITH WHOLE BAKED SWEET POTATOES.

4 tablespoons olive oil
2 onions, roughly chopped
4 garlic cloves, sliced
500g (1lb 2oz) each of minced beef and pork
1 teaspoon sweet smoked paprika
1 tablespoon ground cumin
1 teaspoon ground coriander
1 cinnamon stick
460g (1lb) jar of roasted peppers, drained and
    roughly chopped
2 × 400g (14oz) cans of chopped tomatoes
2 tablespoons ancho chilli paste or chipotle paste
1 teaspoon Worcestershire sauce
salt and black pepper

FOR THE ZESTY CHILLI OIL TOPPER (OPTIONAL)
100ml (3½fl oz) olive oil
3 tablespoons dried chilli flakes
zest of 1 lime
1 tablespoon cumin seeds
1 teaspoon coriander seeds

FOR THE CRUNCHY BEANS (OPTIONAL)
400g (14oz) can of red kidney beans
400g (14oz) can of cannellini beans
2 tablespoons olive oil
1 teaspoon sweet paprika
2 tablespoons maple syrup
salt

TO SERVE
cooked rice or baked sweet potatoes
handful of coriander leaves
lime halves
Our Guacamole (see page 146)
soured cream
grated Cheddar cheese
Mexican hot sauce (Cholula is our favourite)
tortilla chips

SERVES 6

Start with the zesty chilli oil topper, if using. Place all of the ingredients in a small saucepan over a medium heat and gently fry for 3 minutes until sizzling. Remove from the heat and pour into a clean jar. Set aside.

Heat the oil for the chilli in a heavy-based saucepan that has a lid over a low heat. Add the onions and garlic and fry for about 10 minutes until softened.

Increase the heat to high and add both minced meats, along with the paprika, cumin, coriander and cinnamon stick and quickly fry until browned, breaking down any chunks of meat with a wooden spoon. Add the peppers along with with the tomatoes, chilli or chipotle paste and Worcestershire sauce and season well with salt and pepper. Bring to a simmer, cover with a lid and cook over a gentle heat for about 1 hour, stirring occasionally, until the mixture is rich and thickened, removing the lid for the last 10 minutes of cooking.

After about 30 minutes, get on with your crunchy beans, if using. Preheat the oven to 220°C (475°F), Gas Mark 9. Drain and rinse the beans under cold water, then scatter over a large baking sheet. Add the oil, paprika and maple syrup and season well with salt. Toss together until evenly coated. Bake for 30 minutes, tossing the beans every 10 minutes or so, until they are evenly baked and crisp.

Serve the chilli over rice, topped with a sprinkling of beans (or not, in the case of our kids!), a drizzle of zesty chilli oil (if you can) and a scattering of coriander leaves. We also include lime halves, Our Guacamole, soured cream, Cheddar cheese, Mexican hot sauce and tortilla chips for a real feast.

PULLED PORK

SERVES 6–8

OUR BIRTHDAY FEAST OF CHOICE. DELICIOUS, DECADENT, SIMPLE AND FEEDS THE MASSES.
THIS ALSO WORKS AS AN ALTERNATIVE FILLING FOR THE CRISPY FISH TACOS (SEE PAGE 151),
WITH OUR RAINBOW SLAW (SEE PAGE 148), OR EVEN WITH MAC & CHEESE (SEE PAGE 162).
THE POSSIBILITIES ARE ENDLESS.

4 teaspoons sea salt flakes
2 heaped teaspoons smoked
    paprika
1 tablespoon coriander seeds
4 large oranges
4kg (8lb 12 oz) bone-in pork
    shoulder (ask your butcher to
    score the skin 1cm/½ inch deep)
2 limes
3 tablespoons red wine vinegar
10 garlic cloves, peeled
6 bay leaves
3 fresh red chillies
3 tablespoons olive oil

TO SERVE
flour tortillas
onion, finely chopped
Pink Pickled Onions (see page 146)
lime wedges
coriander leaves

Put the salt, paprika, coriander seeds and zest of 1 orange in a bowl
and give it a good mix. Cover the meat with the mixture and place it
on a baking tray. Pop it in the fridge overnight, uncovered – this will
give you the most deliciously moist and crispy pork.

When ready to cook the pork, preheat the oven to its highest setting.

Squeeze the juice of the oranges and limes into a high-sided roasting
tray. Add the red wine vinegar and toss in the garlic, bay leaves and
whole chillies. Place the pork in the middle of the tray, drizzle with
the olive oil and place on the middle shelf of the oven. Immediately
turn the oven down to 160°C (350°F), Gas Mark 4. Roast for 4 hours,
basting occasionally with the juices from the tray. If the fat looks like
it's starting to burn, cover the pork with foil and return to the oven.

Turn the oven down to 140°C (325°F), Gas Mark 3 and continue to
cook for a further 2 hours, or until you can pull the meat apart very
easily with a fork.

Remove the crackling and slice up, then pull all the pork apart,
discarding any bones and fat as you go. Fish out the whole chillies,
slice and place in a bowl for those who like spice. Cover with foil
until ready to serve.

Serve with flour tortillas, finely chopped onion, Pink Pickled
Onions, lime wedges and coriander leaves, as well as cold ginger beer
or ice-cold beers.

STREET CORN

THIS IS A GOOD RECIPE TO BOLSTER ANY BBQS OR COMMUNAL BIG EATS. THE PAPRIKA AND JALAPEÑO BRING A KICK AND THE SWEETCORN BRINGS THE JUICY SWEETNESS.

SERVES 4

6 corn cobs
2 tablespoons butter
1 tablespoon olive oil
1 bunch of spring onions, sliced
juice of 1 lime
1 fresh jalapeño pepper, sliced
    (optional, leave out if you don't
    like it spicy)
handful of coriander, leaves picked and
    chopped, plus extra to serve
2 garlic cloves, grated
100g (3½oz) feta cheese, crumbled
salt and black pepper
pinch of smoked paprika,
    to serve (optional)

Cut the sweetcorn kernels off the cobs into a large bowl. To do this, simply stand the corn upright in the bowl and shave the kernels off the cobs with a small sharp knife.

Melt the butter and oil in a large frying pan over a medium heat. Tip in the corn and fry for about 15 minutes until lightly golden and starting to char in places. You'll need to keep an eye on it, stirring every now and again.

Meanwhile, put the spring onions, lime juice, jalapeño (if using) and coriander in a bowl and stir until combined. Season and set aside.

Add the garlic to the corn and fry for 30 seconds, then turn off the heat.

Tip the corn onto a big serving platter or into a bowl, scatter over the spring onion mixture and finish with crumbled feta and little extra coriander. Sprinkle over a pinch of smoked paprika, too, if you like.

PINK PICKLED ONIONS

MAKES 1 SMALL JAR

2 red onions, finely sliced
pinch of cumin seeds
100ml (3½fl oz) apple cider vinegar
juice of 1 lemon
1 teaspoon salt
1 teaspoon sugar

Place all the ingredients in a mixing bowl and give it all a good scrunch. Transfer to a sterilised 500ml (18fl oz) jar and store for up to a week in the fridge.

OUR GUACAMOLE

SERVES 6 AS A SIDE

1 garlic clove, peeled
3 avocados, halved and stoned
1 onion, finely chopped
1 large tomato, finely chopped
juice of 1 large lime
salt and black pepper

Put the garlic in a large pestle and mortar with a good pinch of salt and bash until smooth. Scoop the avocado flesh out of the halves, add to the mortar and bash until almost smooth. Fold in the chopped onion and tomato and squeeze in the lime juice. Taste and season to your liking.

CORIANDER & JALAPEÑO SALSA

SERVES 6 AS A SIDE

2 bunches of coriander
10 pickled jalapeño chillies
2 garlic cloves, peeled
juice of 2 limes
100ml (3½fl oz) light olive oil
salt and black pepper

TIP
YOU CAN HAVE FUN WITH THE SPICES HERE. I OFTEN CHUCK IN PEPPERCORNS, STAR ANISE, ROSEMARY... WHATEVER I HAVE.

Place all the ingredients in a small blender and blitz until smooth. Taste and adjust the seasoning. Store in a clean jar in the fridge for up to a week. Drizzle over everything. Serve as a dip or a dressing.

TOMATO SALSA

SERVES 6 AS A SIDE

6 ripe tomatoes, finely chopped
1 red onion, finely chopped
1 teaspoon salt
1 teaspoon sugar
zest and juice of 1 lime
small handful of coriander leaves, finely chopped

Place the tomatoes, red onion, salt and sugar in a mixing bowl and leave to marinate for 15 minutes.

Drain the mixture in a fine-mesh sieve, discarding the excess liquid.

Tip back into a bowl, add the lime zest and juice and fold through the chopped coriander.

Rainbow Slaw

THE NAME SAYS IT ALL: A RAINBOW FOR YOUR PLATE AND THE RAW CABBAGE KEEPS IT NICE AND HEALTHY, TOO. REALLY DELICIOUS AND CRUNCHY.

Preheat the oven to 180°C (400°F), Gas Mark 6.

Toss the sweet potatoes and garlic halves onto a large baking tray along with the thyme, olive oil, cumin seeds, sweet paprika and half the cider vinegar. Toss it together so it is all evenly coated, then roast for 20 minutes.

Meanwhile, make the dressing. Simply tip all the ingredients into a clean jar and shake until smooth. Taste and adjust the seasoning.

Remove the baking tray and increase the oven temperature to 220°C (475°F), Gas Mark 9 or as high as it will go. Toss the broccoli into the tray and return it to the oven for 15 minutes.

Put the finely sliced cabbages and coriander stalks and leaves in a large mixing bowl. Season with salt and pepper and toss through the remaining 1 tablespoon of cider vinegar.

When the veg has had its time, the broccoli should have slightly caught but still have a good crunch to it. Toss in everything from the tray into the cabbage and mix it all together. Drizzle over the dressing and serve warm or cold. If you like, serve with a little crumbled feta too.

SERVES 4

2 sweet potatoes, roughly chopped into bite-sized pieces
1 garlic bulb, halved through the middle
½ bunch of thyme
2 tablespoons olive oil
1 tablespoon cumin seeds
1 tablespoon sweet paprika
2 tablespoons apple cider vinegar
1 head of broccoli, roughly chopped
½ red cabbage, finely sliced
½ white cabbage, finely sliced
1 bunch of coriander: stalks finely sliced; leaves torn
salt and black pepper
crumbled feta cheese, to serve (optional)

FOR THE DRESSING
juice of 2 limes
3 tablespoons olive oil
1 tablespoon maple syrup
salt and black pepper

CRISPY FISH TACOS

WE LOVE TACOS AND THESE FISH ONES WORK REALLY WELL. YOU KNOW HOW YOU LIKE THEM BUT WE PILE OURS HIGH WITH THE FISH, GUACAMOLE, SALSA, CHEESE... THE MORE THE MERRIER! GET THAT FLAVOUR IN.

SERVES 4

FOR THE CRISPY FISH
50g (1¾oz) plain flour
50g (1¾oz) cornflour
1 teaspoon baking powder
½ teaspoon sweet paprika
½ teaspoon ground turmeric
75ml (2½fl oz) cold lager
75ml (2½fl oz) cold sparkling water
about 1 litre (1¾ pints) sunflower oil,
    for deep-frying
500g (1lb 2oz) sustainable cod fillets,
    cut into bite-sized chunks
salt and black pepper

FOR THE DRESSING
200g (7oz) mayonnaise
juice of 1 lime
50g (1¾oz) Mexican hot sauce,
    or to taste (optional – subsitute
    for tomato purée or ketchup to
    avoid spice)
½ teaspoon sweet paprika, or to taste

TO SERVE
Our Guacamole (see page 146)
12 corn tacos
Pink Pickled Onions (see page 146)
½ bunch of coriander, leaves picked
    (optional)
lime wedges

To make the crispy fish, in a large mixing bowl, combine the flour, cornflour, baking powder, paprika and turmeric, then season with a good pinch of salt and pepper. Remove 2 heaped tablespoons of the mixture, pop it onto a plate and set aside.

Gradually pour the lager and measured sparkling water into the bowl with the remaining flour mixture, stirring with a whisk until you have a smooth, lump-free batter. Leave to rest for 20 minutes.

Whisk together all the ingredients for the dressing in a separate bowl, taste and adjust the spice to your liking. Feel free to leave out the hot sauce and simply add a squeeze of tomato purée or ketchup if you don't like the heat.

Place a large heavy-based saucepan over a medium heat and pour in enough oil to fill the pan by one third. Heat to 180–190°C (350–375°F), or until a drop of the batter sizzles and crisps up as soon as it is added.

Toss the fish chunks in the reserved flour mixture, shake off any excess, then dip each piece into the batter. Carefully lower each piece into the hot oil and fry for 3–4 minutes, or until golden and crisp. You'll need to do this in batches, ensuring you don't overcrowd the pan. Remove with a slotted spoon to drain on kitchen paper.

When ready to serve, spread a little of Our Guacamole on each taco, spoon on a few Pink Pickled Onions, top with the crispy fish and add a good sprinkling of dressing. Finish with some fresh coriander, if you like, and serve with lime wedges for squeezing.

Pictured overleaf ☞

corn cake

OUR FAVOURITE KIND OF SWEET TREAT IS ACTUALLY…
NOT TOO SWEET, SO THIS SLIGHTLY SAVOURY CORN
CAKE IS JUST RIGHT. YOU'LL BE A CONVERT WE PROMISE.
ALSO, IT'S NICE AND EASY TO MAKE.

Preheat the oven to 170°C (375°F), Gas Mark 5. Grease and line a
22cm (8½ inch) springform cake tin with baking paper.

Place the corn in a food processor and blend until smooth.
Add the remaining cake ingredients and blend until everything
is well combined.

Pour the mixture into the prepared tin and use the back of a spoon
to level it out.

Bake for 30 minutes or until an inserted skewer comes out clean.
Remove from the oven and leave to cool for 10 minutes.

Meanwhile, mix together the lime juice, icing sugar and vanilla
bean paste until you have a thick and smooth icing.

Remove the cake from the tin and drizzle over the icing. Serve
warm, with a dollop of crème fraîche, if you like.

FOR THE CAKE
100g (3½oz) unsalted butter, melted,
    plus extra to grease the cake tin
500g (1lb 2oz) fresh sweetcorn kernels
2 tablespoons soft brown sugar
75g (2¾oz) plain flour
3 large free-range eggs
1 tablespoon baking powder
½ teaspoon salt
zest of 2 limes

TO DECORATE
juice of 2 limes
4 tablespoons icing sugar
½ teaspoon vanilla bean paste

TO SERVE (OPTIONAL)
crème fraîche

new♥ aMERICa STYLE

When we were kids, America was literally the most glamorous place to us. We have both been lucky enough to tour the USA with our music and it's somewhere we've had so many fun experiences. These recipes keep the memories alive!

FRIED CHICKEN & OUR PERFECT CHIPS

SERVE WITH A ZINGY SLAW AND SWEETCORN, IF YOU FANCY.

SERVES 6

FOR OUR PERFECT CHIPS
1kg (2lb 4oz) potatoes (Maris Piper
   or russet potatoes)
about 1 litre (1¾ pints) groundnut
   oil, for deep-frying
6 rosemary sprigs
1 garlic bulb, bashed
sea salt flakes

FOR THE CHICKEN
200g (7oz) full-fat mayonnaise
100g (3½oz) cornflour
1 teaspoon each of sweet paprika,
   garlic granules, salt and cracked
   black pepper
200g (7oz) panko breadcrumbs
5 boneless skin-on chicken breasts,
   halved

TO SERVE (OPTIONAL)
slaw
corn on the cob

Start with preparing the chips. Peel and slice the potatoes for your chips to whatever thickness you like. We like skinny fries in our house. Tip the sliced potatoes onto a clean tea towel and dry as thoroughly as possible. Cover and set aside.

Pour the oil for deep-frying into a large heavy-based saucepan and set over a medium heat. Add the rosemary sprigs and bashed garlic – this will lightly flavour the oil and also help prevent the house smelling of oil. If you are like us and bought a deep-fat fryer during lockdown, use that instead, obviously. Bring the oil to 170°C (340°F). If you don't have a thermometer, the oil needs to gently bubble as you fry the chicken. Don't be tempted to whack the heat up, as the outside of the chicken will burn quickly and the inside won't cook.

To prepare the chicken, scoop the mayo onto a plate. Mix the cornflour, sweet paprika, garlic granules, salt, pepper and breadcrumbs in a separate bowl. Dip each chicken piece into the mayo, using a spoon to smear a thin coating all over. Toss into the flour mixture, giving it a bash against the bowl to remove any excess flour. Place on a large baking tray until everything is coated. Preheat the oven to 140°C (325°F), Gas Mark 3.

Working in batches of 4 at a time, gently lower the chicken into the hot oil. Fry for 6–8 minutes, turning halfway so each piece is evenly golden. Remove with a slotted spoon to a separate large baking tray until you have fried all the chicken. Pop the tray into the oven for 10 minutes while you cook the chips.

Add half of the chips to the hot oil and fry until very lightly golden. Remove with a slotted spoon to a large colander. Season with salt and toss to remove excess oil, then tip onto a baking tray. Fry the remaining potatoes in the same way. Add the first batch back into the hot oil and fry once more until just golden and perfectly crisp. Remove as before and toss with salt. Repeat with the last batch and pop them all into a large serving dish for the table.

Remove the chicken from the oven and serve immediately, with a sharp zingy slaw and some corn on the cobs, if you like.

Pictured overleaf ☞

MAC & CHEESE
WITH CRUNCHY SAGE BREADCRUMB TOPPING

A CLASSIC! I DON'T KNOW ANYONE WHO DOESN'T ADORE THIS. INDULGENT LOVE ON A PLATE.

SERVES 8

150g (5½oz) salted butter
5 garlic cloves, finely sliced
6 tablespoons plain flour
1½ tablespoons English
    mustard powder
1 teaspoon smoked paprika
6 bay leaves
2 litres (generous 3½ pints)
    semi-skimmed milk
600g (1lb 5oz) dried macaroni
300g (10½oz) Cheddar cheese, grated
100g (3½oz) Parmesan cheese, grated
200g (7oz) panko breadcrumbs
15 sage leaves
150g (5½oz) ball of mozzarella
olive oil, for drizzling
salt and black pepper

TO SERVE (OPTIONAL)
crisp salad
Fried Chicken (see page 158)
Boston Beans (see page 174)

Preheat the oven to 200°C (425°F), Gas Mark 7.

Put the butter and garlic in a large saucepan and melt over a medium heat, then add the flour and stir until incorporated. Add the mustard powder, paprika and bay leaves, reduce the heat and cook, stirring continuously, for 5 minutes. Gradually pour in the milk, whisking as you go to avoid lumps. Bring the sauce to the boil, then leave it over a low heat to simmer, making sure you stir it often.

Meanwhile, bring a large pan of salted water to a rapid boil over a high heat. Add the pasta and cook for 6 minutes.

Remove the bay leaves from the sauce, then drain the pasta and add it to the sauce. Remove from the heat, give it a good stir and add two-thirds of the grated cheeses. Season well with salt and pepper to taste.

Tip the mixture into a 30 × 20cm (12 × 8 inch) baking dish, scatter over the breadcrumbs and place the sage leaves on top. Scatter over the remaining grated cheese and tear the mozzarella on top. Drizzle with olive oil.

Bake for 30 minutes, or until golden and crispy on top.

Serve this on its own, with a crisp salad or, for utter decadence, with Fried Chicken and Boston Beans.

SOUTHERN CRAB FEAST WITH CHORIZO, CORN, BAKED POTATOES & A BUTTER DRIZZLE

IF YOU CAN'T GET WHOLE CRABS, USE DRESSED CRAB AND, INSTEAD OF ADDING IT TO THE STOCK, SIMPLY REHEAT IN IN THE PAN WITH THE HOT BUTTER DRIZZLE.

SERVES 6

3 live cock (male) crabs
150g (5½oz) chorizo, cut into 2cm (¾ inch) pieces
3 onions, each cut through the root into 8 wedges
3 corn cobs, leaves removed, halved
6 bay leaves
1 teaspoon celery salt
1 teaspoon English mustard powder
¼ teaspoon allspice
½ teaspoon cayenne pepper
1.5 litres (generous 2½ pints) pale ale
1.5 litres (generous 2½ pints) water
salt and black pepper
lemon wedges, to serve

FOR THE BAKED POTATOES
6 baking potatoes
2 tablespoons olive oil
salt

FOR THE HOT BUTTER DRIZZLE
200g (7oz) unsalted butter
1 small bunch of thyme, leaves picked
1 small bunch of flat leaf parsley, finely chopped
zest of 1 lemon
2 garlic cloves, finely chopped
salt and black pepper

Preheat the oven to 200°C (425°F), Gas Mark 7.

Start with the baked potatoes. Prick the potatoes with a fork, rub with the olive oil and sprinkle with salt. Place directly on the oven shelf and bake for 50 minutes, then increase the oven temperature to 220°C (475°F), Gas Mark 9 and cook for a further 15 minutes until golden and crisp on the outside and fluffy inside.

Meanwhile, put the crabs into the freezer for 10 minutes to stun them before you need them for cooking. Next, fry the chorizo in a large, heavy-based saucepan over a medium-low heat to render out the fat, then pour the fat into a bowl and set aside. Add the onions to the pan along with the corn cobs, bay leaves, celery salt, spices, a good pinch of salt, the pale ale and measured water. Bring to the boil, then reduce to a simmer and cook for 12–15 minutes until the corn is tender. Using a slotted spoon or tongs, lift the onions, corn and chorizo from the liquid and transfer to a tray. Add the crabs to the stock left in the pan and cook for 10–15 minutes, depending on their size.

As the crab cooks, make the hot butter drizzle. Melt the butter in a small saucepan over a low heat, then mix in the reserved chorizo oil, herbs, lemon zest and garlic. Season to taste.

Remove the crabs from the stock, twist off the legs and claws and set aside. Very firmly press your thumbs on either side of the eyes to push away the body from the shell. Remove and discard the feathery gills. Cut the main body in half and remove the white meat from the crevices of the main body with a skewer. Remove the greyish stomach sac from the shell and discard. Use a spoon to scrape the brown meat from the shell into a bowl. Bash the claws and legs with a rolling pin to crack the shells and remove the meat inside. Check the collected white and brown meat for any shards of

shell before mixing together and returning to the crab shell
to serve.

To serve, arrange the crab, corn, onions and chorizo on a large tray
or platter. Drizzle over the hot butter and serve with the baked
potatoes and lemon wedges on the side.

Pictured overleaf ☞

BBQ TUNA BURGERS WITH WASABI MAYO & SWEET POTATO FRIES

WE LOVE A BEEF BURGER, BUT THIS IS OUR FAVOURITE ALTERNATIVE. IT CARRIES YOU TO A WHOLE NEW PLACE WITH THE FLAVOURS. EAT ON A SUNNY DAY AND PRETEND YOU'RE IN LA!

SERVES 4

4 × 125g (4½oz) tuna steaks
2 tablespoons olive oil
4 burger buns, sliced in half
salt and black pepper

FOR THE SWEET POTATO FRIES
4 sweet potatoes, cut lengthways into
   2cm (¾ inch) wedges
2 tablespoons olive oil
2 tablespoons semolina
salt and black pepper

FOR THE WASABI MAYO
100g (3½oz) good-quality mayonnaise
1 tablespoon wasabi
juice of ½ lime

TO SERVE
crunchy lettuce leaves
sliced avocado
kimchi
coriander leaves (optional)

Preheat the oven to 200°C (425°F), Gas Mark 7.

Start with the fries. Toss the sweet potato wedges with the olive oil, semolina and a pinch of salt and pepper. Spread over a large baking tray and roast for 20–25 minutes until golden and crisp.

Meanwhile, mix the wasabi mayo ingredients together in a small bowl and taste for seasoning.

About 10 minutes before the potatoes are done, lightly brush the tuna steaks with the olive oil, a sprinkle of salt and a good grind of black pepper.

Make sure the BBQ is at its most scorching hot (or use a griddle pan on the hob if it's a rainy day). Sear the tuna steaks for 2–3 minutes on each side until just pink in the middle, or longer if you prefer. Set aside on a plate to rest briefly while you lightly toast the burger buns on the griddle.

Slather the inside of the burger buns with the wasabi mayo, tuck in the tuna steak along with some lettuce leaves, sliced avocado, kimchi and coriander leaves, if you like. Serve with the sweet potato wedges.

BBQ SaUCE RIBS
WITH PICKLED SLaW

SERVES 6–8

THIS IS GREAT SERVED WITH BAKED POTATOES (SEE PAGE 164) OR MAC & CHEESE (SEE PAGE 162).

FOR THE RIBS
4 racks of baby back pork ribs
(about 1.25kg/2lb 12oz)
1 litre (1¾ pints) cola
1 teaspoon garlic powder
1 teaspoon onion powder
1 teaspoon sweet paprika
1 teaspoon salt
1 teaspoon cracked black pepper

FOR THE PICKLED SLAW
200g (7oz) kale or Brussels sprouts
(optional)
¼ red cabbage
1 red onion
2 tablespoons white wine vinegar,
or to taste
1 teaspoon sea salt flakes, or to taste
2 carrots
2 teaspoons Dijon mustard
2 tablespoons olive oil
200g (7oz) crème fraîche
10 cornichons

FOR THE BBQ SAUCE
200g (7oz) tomato ketchup
200g (7oz) soft brown sugar
4 tablespoons Worcestershire sauce
1 tablespoon sweet paprika
200ml (7fl oz) apple juice
2 tablespoons English mustard
1 teaspoon cracked black pepper
1 teaspoon salt

Preheat the oven to 160°C (350°F), Gas Mark 4.

Place the ribs in a large high-sided roasting tray. Ideally, they will be snug but not overlapping. Pour over the cola and the remaining rib ingredients and give it all a good toss. Pour in just enough water to cover the ribs. Cover the whole tray with foil and roast for 3 hours, turning the tray halfway through.

An hour before the ribs are ready, make the slaw. You can also make it ahead and refrigerate until ready to serve. Shred the kale or Brussels sprouts, if using, into thin strips (separating out the sprouts a bit) and place in a large serving bowl. Finely slice the red cabbage and the onion and add to the bowl with the kale. Pour over the vinegar, add the salt and give it a really good scrunch. Using a julienne peeler or grater, grate in the carrots. Add the mustard, oil and crème fraîche and mix it all together. Roughly chop the cornichons and sprinkle over the top. Taste and add a little more salt or vinegar, if needed. Set aside.

Now make the BBQ sauce – this can also be made ahead and kept in a jar. Simply put all the ingredients in a medium pan and place over a low heat for 10 minutes, or until all the ingredients have combined and sugar has melted. Remove from the heat and set aside.

When the ribs are done, remove from the tray and pour away the liquid. Put the ribs back into the tray and cover with half of the sauce, rubbing it all over so all the ribs are evenly coated. Cover and chill for at least an hour. If you have time, 24 hours is ideal.

Increase the oven temperature to 220°C (475°F), Gas Mark 9.

Return the ribs to the oven and cook for a final 20 minutes, turning occasionally. You want the sauce to catch slightly and the ribs should be nice and hot throughout.

Slice up the ribs and serve with slaw and the remaining sauce on the side.

BOSTON BEANS ON SOURDOUGH

WARMING AND SATISFYING, A FANCIER TWIST ON 'BEANS ON TOAST' AND SUPER SIMPLE TO MAKE, TOO.

SERVES 4–6

2 tablespoons olive oil
2 tablespoons salted butter
6 smoked streaky bacon rashers, roughly chopped into 2cm (¾ inch) chunks
1 large onion, finely chopped
4 garlic cloves, sliced
3 thyme sprigs
1 tablespoon sweet paprika
1 teaspoon red wine vinegar
400g (14oz) can of haricot beans
400g (14oz) can of cannellini beans
400g (14oz) can of chopped tomatoes
2 tablespoons soft brown sugar
4 dashes of Worcestershire sauce
salt and black pepper

TO SERVE
8–12 slices of sourdough toast
butter, for spreading

Heat the olive oil and butter in a medium heavy-based saucepan over a medium heat, add the bacon and fry until golden and crisp. Scoop out with a slotted spoon and set aside.

Add the onion and garlic to the same pan and fry for 3 minutes, or until soft and translucent. Add the thyme, sweet paprika and red wine vinegar and fry for a further 2 minutes.

Drain the beans in a colander and rinse under cold water, then add to the pan with the tomatoes, brown sugar and Worcestershire sauce. Leave to simmer for 20 minutes, stirring often.

Season with salt and pepper to taste.

Toast your bread and smoother in butter. Serve 2 slices per plate, topped with a spoonful of beans and with the crispy bacon crumbled over. Eat immediately.

CORN CHOWDER

THIS IS A RELATIVELY NEW ADDITION TO OUR HOME TABLE BUT IT'S ALREADY A FAVOURITE. SO DELICIOUS AND HEARTY.

SERVES 4–6

500g (1lb 2oz) baby new potatoes
1 large knob of butter
2 tablespoons olive oil
150g (5½oz) diced pancetta
4 leeks, halved and sliced into 2cm
   (¾ inch) half-moons
3 garlic cloves, sliced
5 thyme sprigs
½ teaspoon sweet smoked paprika
300ml (10fl oz) white wine
300ml (10fl oz) chicken or veg stock
400ml (14fl oz) single cream
5 bay leaves
300g (10½oz) smoked haddock
200g (7oz) fresh or frozen
   sweetcorn kernels
½ bunch of flat leaf parsley,
   roughly chopped
salt and black pepper

TO SERVE
warm bread
1 lemon, cut into wedges

Roughly chop any large baby potatoes and keep the small ones whole. Add to a medium saucepan, cover with water, season with salt and place over a medium heat. Boil for about 20 minutes until soft in the middle, then drain and set aside.

Meanwhile, heat the butter and oil in a large heavy-based saucepan over a high heat, add the pancetta and fry until lightly golden, then chuck in the leeks and garlic, reduce the heat to medium, and fry for about 5 minutes until the leeks are soft. Add the thyme and paprika and fry for a further minute, then pour in the wine and cook for 5 minutes. Pour in the stock and cream, add the bay leaves and simmer for 5 minutes, then add the cooked potatoes and simmer for 10 minutes.

Chop the smoked haddock into bite-sized pieces and add to the pan along with the sweetcorn. Cook for a further 6 minutes. Season well with salt and pepper and stir through the parsley.

Ladle into bowls and serve with warm bread and lemon wedges.

auntie martha's giant cookie cake

SERVES 6–8

AUNTIE MARTHA IS OUR RESIDENT FAMILY BAKER.
HER GIANT COOKIE CAKE ALWAYS MEANS A SUPERSIZE
CELEBRATION – THAT'S HOW THE COOKIE CRUMBLES!

FOR THE CAKE
275g (9¾oz) plain flour
1 teaspoon bicarbonate of soda
1 teaspoon sea salt flakes
115g (4oz) unsalted butter
55g (2oz) golden caster sugar
140g (5oz) light brown soft sugar
1 large free-range egg
1 teaspoon vanilla extract
100g (3½oz) milk chocolate, roughly chopped
100g (3½oz) white chocolate, roughly chopped

FOR THE BUTTERCREAM
100g (3½oz) unsalted butter (at room temperature)
125g (4½oz) icing sugar
1 teaspoon vanilla bean paste
1 tablespoon milk
natural food colouring (optional)

TO DECORATE
melted chocolate
sprinkles
candles

Preheat the oven to 180°C (400°F), Gas Mark 6. Line a 20cm (8 inch) round cake tin with baking paper.

In a large bowl, mix together the flour, bicarbonate of soda and salt. Set aside.

Melt the butter in a small saucepan over a medium heat. Pour it into a separate large heatproof mixing bowl and mix in the sugars until the mixture is smooth. Crack in the egg and add the vanilla, then briefly whisk again until you have a lovely, smooth, glossy mixture.

Using a wooden spoon, mix the dry ingredients into the wet mixture, then fold through the chocolate and mix until you have a thick cookie-like dough.

Press the mixture into the lined tin, evenly pressing into the sides. Bake for 20 minutes, or until lightly golden and just set.

Leave the cookie to cool for about 10 minutes in the tin, then pop out and place on a plate.

Once the cookie has completely cooled, make the buttercream. In a large bowl, beat the butter with an electric mixer until pale and fluffy, about 5 minutes. Sift in the icing sugar, add the vanilla paste and milk and beat again until smooth.

For a fancy multi-coloured icing, separate the buttercream into 3 (or how ever many colours you'd like) different bowls and add a different colouring to each. Add each to separate piping bags and then open up a spare piping bag and lay flat. Pipe a thick line of each colour along the length of the flat bag, then reassemble the bag with the 3 colours in, add a star nozzle, and pipe decoratively around the edge. (Or for a simple life, just stick to one colour and pipe the buttercream all the way around the edge of the cookie, and use it to write a message in the middle!)

Sprinkle with colourful sprinkles and serve, with candles if you like.

KIDS CREATE♥ FEAST

This is the stuff our bosses – oops, sorry, I mean our kids – like to eat. If we left them in control of the kitchen, this is what they'd make. Often simple, sometimes messy and always tasty. The meals that childhood food memories are made of.

BUILD-YOUR-OWN pancakes

THIS IS ALSO KNOWN AS 'SATURDAY MORNING BREAKFAST'. IT'S LIKE CLOCKWORK, AND ACTUALLY WE LOVE MAKING THEM. THE SIMPLE ALCHEMY OF BATTER IN, GOLDEN PANCAKE OUT, MAKES OUR HEARTS HAPPY EVERY TIME.

200g (7oz), or 1 mug, of self-raising flour
400ml (14fl oz), or 1 mug, of milk
2 free-range eggs
unsalted butter, for frying

OPTIONAL TOPPINGS
chocolate hazelnut spread
blueberries
raspberries
chocolate flakes
toasted nuts
chopped fruit
fave cereal
yogurt
maple syrup
YOU DO YOU

MAKES 12–15

Place the flour in a bowl and pour in the milk (we find using the same mug to measure consistent quantities of them out to be the simplest option). Then crack in the eggs and whisk until you have a lovely smooth batter.

Place a large pan over a medium heat and add a little knob of butter. Swirl until the melted butter evenly covers the base of the pan. Depending on your pan size you might be able to make only 2 pancakes at a time. Plus, if you have any fun heatproof moulds, feel free to use them, placing them in the pan at this point. Ladle in about 2 tablespoons of the batter, then ladle in a second 2 tablespoons of batter a little further away, so the pancakes have space to grow. Cook for 1 minute, then use a spatula to flip the pancakes. They should be golden and set on the bottom and easy enough to flip, but if they aren't flipping easily, cook for a bit longer before flipping next time.

Continue to add a little extra butter each time you add new pancakes to the pan.

Serve immediately with whatever you fancy on top, or keep warm in a low oven while you fry the rest and enjoy them all together.

TIP
YOU CAN ALSO FREEZE
THESE. JUST DEFROST
IN A SINGLE LAYER IN
THE MICROWAVE.

SPEEDY PASTA SAUCES

THE KIDS' TOP PASTA SAUCES AND THE ONES THEIR FRIENDS ASK FOR WHEN THEY COME OVER TO PLAY. GOOD TOO FOR ENCOURAGING CONFIDENCE IN THE KITCHEN AS THEY ALL GET THESE UNDER THEIR BELTS RELATIVELY YOUNG. YES, THEY ARE QUITE SIMPLE BUT THEREIN LIES THE BEAUTY. WHEN YOU GET IT RIGHT, A SIMPLE TOMATO SAUCE IS THE BEST THING YOU'VE EVER EATEN AND THE ONLY FOOD YOU WANT. SO, COURTESY OF SONNY, KIT, RAY, JESSE AND MICKEY, HERE ARE THEIR PASTA SAUCES.

CROWD-PLEASING PASTA

SERVES 4

200g (7oz) pasta of your choice
sauce of choice (see following pages)
salt
grated Parmesan or Cheddar cheese, to serve

Bring a pan of salted water to the boil. Cook the pasta according to the packet instructions. Drain and serve with sauce tossed through, or simply with a grating of Parmesan or Cheddar cheese, if your little ones like it.

KIT'S ALMOND PESTO

SERVES 4

30g (1oz) pine nuts
30g (1oz) almonds
1 large bunch of basil (about 100g/3½oz),
    plus extra leaves to serve
60g (2¼oz) Parmesan cheese, roughly chopped
100ml (3½fl oz) olive oil, plus extra to serve
2 garlic cloves
juice of 1 lemon
salt and black pepper

Heat a small frying pan over a low heat.
Toast the pine nuts until golden, shaking
occasionally for an even colour. Once done,
set aside a handful to serve.

Add all the rest of the ingredients to a blender
and pulse until you have a smooth paste. Taste
and season a little.

Stir through any cooked pasta of your choice
and serve sprinkled with the reserved toasted
pine nuts, a few basil leaves and an extra
drizzle of olive oil.

FRESH CHERRY TOMATO SAUCE

SERVES 4

300g (10½oz) cherry tomatoes, quartered
1 garlic clove, peeled
100ml (3½fl oz) olive oil
juice of ½ lemon
pinch of salt

Place the tomatoes in a large bowl, grate in the
garlic, add the oil and squeeze over the lemon
juice. Season with a pinch of salt and toss to
combine well.

Once your pasta is cooked, toss into the bowl with
the sauce and serve.

SIMPLE POMODORO sauce

2 tablespoons olive oil
2 garlic cloves, sliced
400g (14oz) can of chopped tomatoes or
    whole cherry tomatoes
handful of basil leaves, finely chopped
salt

Heat the oil in a large frying pan over a medium heat, add the garlic and fry until lightly golden. Add the tomatoes and simmer for 10 minutes, stirring every now and again. Stir through the basil and season with a little salt to taste, then stir through any cooked pasta of your choice and serve.

SIMPLE PESTO

SERVES 4

30g (1oz) pine nuts
1 bunch of basil
60g (2¼oz) Parmesan cheese, roughly chopped,
    plus extra, finely grated, to serve
100ml (3½fl oz) olive oil
2 garlic cloves
salt and black pepper

Heat a small frying pan over a low heat. Toss in the pine nuts and toast until golden, shaking the pan occasionally so they get an even colour.

Add all the ingredients to a blender and pulse until you have a smooth paste. Taste and season a little.

Stir through any cooked pasta of your choice and serve with extra finely grated Parmesan.

PIZZA TIME!

THE KIDS GET VERY EXCITED WHEN IT'S PIZZA TIME AND THEY ALL LIKE ADDING THEIR OWN FAVOURITE TOPPINGS. IT TURNS INTO A LITTLE CONVEYOR BELT OPERATION ONCE PAPA JONES HAS THE GOZNEY PIZZA OVEN (A 40TH BIRTHDAY PRESENT FROM GRANDMA AND GRANDPA) FIRED UP! IF YOU DON'T HAVE ONE, AN OVEN WILL DO THE JOB, TOO.

SERVES 4

400g (14oz) can of plum tomatoes
large pinch of dried oregano
3 garlic cloves, peeled
1 tablespoon semolina
100g (3½oz) grated mozzarella
125g (4½oz) mozzarella ball, drained
1 bunch of basil
olive oil, for drizzling
salt

PIZZA DOUGH (OR USE DEFROSTED FROZEN PIZZA DOUGHBALLS)
1 teaspoon fast-action dried yeast
pinch of caster sugar
500g (1lb) plain flour, plus extra for dusting
350ml (12fl oz) lukewarm water
1½ teaspoons salt

OTHER TOPPING OPTIONS
sliced chorizo sausage
ham
sliced red onion
sliced mushrooms

To make the pizza dough, put the yeast and sugar in a large bowl with 2 tablespoons of the flour and 50ml (2fl oz) of the measured water. Let stand until bubbles form, about 5 minutes, then add the remaining water, the salt and half the remaining flour. Stir until you have a paste-like mixture. Then gradually add the remaining flour until you have a moist dough. Shape the dough into a ball, cover with a damp cloth and leave to rest in a warm place for 5 minutes. Turn out onto a lightly floured work surface and knead for 10 minutes until smooth and elastic. Lightly oil the mixing bowl and return the dough to the bowl. Cover with a damp cloth and leave to rise in a warm place for 1 hour.

When the dough has risen, preheat the oven to 220°C (475°F), Gas Mark 9, or as high as your oven will go.

Place the tomatoes, garlic and oregano in a blender and blitz into a smooth tomato sauce. Season with a little salt and set aside.

Sprinkle the work surface with flour and a little semolina (this will help the pizza not to stick). Separate the dough into 4 pieces then roll it out into 4 rounds, each roughly 25cm (10 inches) in diameter. Place the rounds onto your largest baking trays. Ideally, you have 2 trays and 2 pizzas will fit on both, but if not just reuse the trays once each pizza is cooked.

Add about 2 tablespoons of the tomato sauce onto each pizza base and smear it around, leaving a 3cm (1 inch) border. Top each with an equal amount of grated mozzarella cheese then tear up the mozzarella balls and place the pieces randomly across each pizza (not too much or it will get soggy). Our kids love doing this. Obviously, have fun adding your own toppings. Our kids all have different things they want to add, from chorizo slices or ham to onion and mushrooms.

Bake for 6–8 minutes, or until the dough is golden and crisp. To finish, remove from the oven, top with a few basil leaves and a drizzle of olive oil. Slice up and serve.

ULTIMATE FISH FINGER SANDWICH

GO POSH, IF YOU LIKE, BUT WE LIKE THE CLASSIC BIRDS EYE VERSION IN OUR HOUSE.

**8 frozen fish fingers of
your choice**
8 slices of white farmhouse bread
enough butter for 4 slices of bread
1 Gem lettuce

FOR OUR FISH FINGER SAUCE
2 tablespoon capers
8 cornichons
4 tablespoons mayonnaise

FOR THE SMASHED PEAS
250g (9oz) frozen peas
2 tablespoons crème fraîche
juice of ½ lemon
a pinch of salt

SERVES 4 (BUT CAN EASILY BE HALVED)

Cook the fish fingers according to the packet instructions, or until golden and crisp. There is nothing worse than a soggy fish finger.

Meanwhile, place a medium pan filled with water over a high heat.

While the water comes to the boil, make our fish finger sauce. Simply chop up the capers and cornichons and place in a bowl with the mayonnaise. Mix together and set aside.

When the water is boiling, add the peas and and boil for 2 minutes, then drain and toss into a food processor along with the crème fraîche, lemon juice and salt. Blitz until you have a coarse mixture. This pea mixture works in the sandwich but is very messy to eat! Serve it alongside if you prefer.

When the fish fingers are ready, remove from the oven and leave to cool slightly.

Butter 4 slices of bread, then smear a little of the fish finger sauce over each slice. Top each with 2 fish fingers, dollop a little of the smashed peas on top and place a couple of Gem lettuce leaves on top of that. Top with the remaining bread slices. Slice in half and serve.

STICKY HONEY & MUSTARD SAUSAGES WITH SMASHED SWEET POTATOES

STICKY, YES, BUT SO DELICIOUS. CAN BE MADE WITH VEGETARIAN SAUSAGES FOR THE NON-MEAT EATERS, BUT THE FLAVOUR IS A WINNER WITH ALL.

SERVES 4 LITTLE MONSTERS

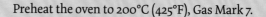

4 tablespoons runny honey
4 tablespoons wholegrain mustard
2 red onions, each sliced into 8 wedges
8 chipolata sausages
2 tablespoons olive oil

FOR THE MASH
4 sweet potatoes, roughly chopped
100g (3½oz) butter
salt

TO SERVE
ketchup
peas or wilted greens

Preheat the oven to 200°C (425°F), Gas Mark 7.

In a small bowl, mix together the honey and mustard.

Place the onion wedges and sausages on a large baking tray. Pour over the honey and mustard mixture and give it all a good toss. Drizzle over the oil.

Roast for 25–30 minutes, tossing halfway through, or until the sausages are sticky and cooked through.

Meanwhile, bring a medium pan of water to the boil over a high heat. Add the sweet potatoes and boil for about 15 minutes until soft. Drain and leave to dry a little, then return the cooked potatoes to the pan and add the butter. Give it a good mash and season a little with salt.

When the sausages are ready, serve with a good dollop of the mash, some ketchup and peas or wilted greens.

★ BEDTIME

YOU SHOULD BE IN BE
TOAST WITH BUTTER
" HOUMOUS

RICE CAKES

ALMONDS

BANANA

➡ DRINKS

WARM MILK

★ BE POLITE OR N
(MENU CAN CHANGE A

CAFÉ

ACKS ★

TOAST
MARMITE

OURS:A.306M - 9PM

SERVICE ★

MGMT SEES FIT)

a BUG'S LIFE

SO-NAMED BECAUSE OF THE CARTOON THAT WAS PLAYING WHEN WE WANTED SONNY TO EAT SOMETHING. WE NAMED THIS SANDWICH AFTER THE FILM SO HE'D EAT, AND IT WORKED. WORKED REALLY WELL! HE STILL EATS IT NOW.

FEEDS 1 LITTLE BUG

2 slices of sliced white bread
knob of butter
1 tablespoon mango chutney
50g (1¾oz) Cheddar cheese, grated

Place a large frying pan over a medium heat. While it is heating up, butter both slices of the bread on one side each. Smear the mango chutney over the unbuttered side of one of the pieces of bread and top with the grated cheese. Place the slice, buttered-side down, in the hot pan and top with the remaining slice of bread, this one buttered-side up. Squish down with a spatula and fry for 3 minutes, or until golden and crisp, then flip and fry the other side.

Slice in half and serve. Careful – the cheese is melty hot!

YOU-SHOULD-BE-IN-BED TOAST

YEP, THIS BRUSCHETTA IS WHAT WE'D MAKE FOR THE KIDS (KIT ESPECIALLY) WHEN THEY WOULD COME DOWN AFTER BEDTIME AND CLAIM TO BE STILL HUNGRY. YOU REALLY SHOULD HAVE BEEN IN BED, BUT WE MADE YOU TOMATO TOAST.

SERVES 2 LITTLE RAVERS

2 slices of bread (use your
    kids' fave)
150g (5½oz) cherry tomatoes
1 tablespoon olive oil
a few basil leaves (optional)
sprinkle of salt

Toast the bread.

While the bread is toasting, chop the tomatoes into halves and place in a bowl. Sprinkle with salt, drizzle over the oil and tear in a little basil, if your little ones like it.

Scoop the tomatoes onto the toast and serve.

Unikorn
Flakes

SERVES 8

nanny claire's cadbury's tribute cake

CLAIRE'S LASTING LEGACY FOR TIME ETERNAL I THINK: HER INFAMOUS TRIBUTE CAKE. THE REAL ONE USES EVEN MORE CHOCOLATE BUT WE'D PROBABLY GET IN TROUBLE FOR ENCOURAGING IT. WHICHEVER WAY YOU DO IT, SPONGE + CHOCOLATE + CHOCOLATE DECORATIONS = FUN ON A PLATE. HAPPY BIRTHDAY! (EAT EVEN IF IT'S NOT YOUR BIRTHDAY.)

FOR THE CAKE
350g (12oz) unsalted butter, softened
200g (7oz) granulated sugar
280g (10oz) self-raising flour
55g (2oz) Cadbury's cocoa
6 free-range eggs

FOR THE TOPPING
200g (7oz) Cadbury's Dairy Milk
tub of Cadbury's Roses (or Heroes)
Cadbury's Chocolate Spread

Line 2 × 20cm (8 inch) cake tins with baking paper. Heat the oven to 140°C (325°F), Gas Mark 3.

Cream together the butter and sugar with an electric whisk. Add the remaining cake ingredients and mix until you have a smooth batter. Pour the batter into the 2 lined cake tins and bake in the middle of the oven until springy to touch, about 30 minutes.

When the cakes are cooked, remove from the oven and allow to cool in the tins for a few minutes, before turning out onto a wire rack to cool completely.

Meanwhile break up the Cadbury's Dairy Milk into squares and place on a plate. Unwrap the Roses or Heroes (do not trust the children with this task).

When the cakes are cooled, level out the bottom of one cake and spread the Cadbury's Chocolate Spread across the top of the cake, then carefully place the other cake on top.

Melt the chocolate squares in the microwave for 1–2 minutes, until soft but not runny. Spoon the melted chocolate on top of the cake and allow it to dribble down the sides. When the chocolate is semi-set, decorate the top the cake with the individual chocolates. Serve immediately, this is best eaten before the chocolate is fully set.

cave baby

INSPIRED BY A SMOOTHIE WE HAD AT A THEME PARK IN MEXICO, THIS IS DELICIOUS AND FUN TO MAKE.

SERVES 2

2 bananas, peeled
500ml (16fl oz) milk of your choice
1 teaspoon agave syrup
handful of ice

Add all the ingredients to a small blender and blitz until smooth. Pour into glasses and serve with straws, umbrellas or simply on its own.

KITCHEN DISCO♥ COCKTAILS

We've always had a place in our hearts for cocktails, but during our months of kitchen discos we fell even more in love with them and expanded the repertoire. A cocktail is clever, it adds a layer of retro glamour to the proceedings and turns a Friday night in into a party night. Whether toasting a big event or just making it to the weekend... Cheers!

OUR LOVE OF COCKTAILS

Making cocktails is all about ratios and is much easier than you would think. We recommend getting yourself a cocktail jigger which always has a 2:1 measure (a double at one end – usually 50ml/2fl oz, a single at the other – usually 25ml/1fl oz). This makes it quick and easy to make yourself whatever you fancy. So, when following these recipes, 100ml (3½fl oz) means two big ones and 50 ml (2fl oz) is one, leaving 25ml (1fl oz) as one of the small measures. If it says 40ml (scant 3 tablespoons) you can approximate. It's all going to end up tasting delicious. Enjoy.

MURDER ON THE DANCE FLOOR

WELL IT WAS ONLY A MATTER OF TIME! BLOOD RED AND MADE WITH OUR OWN BOTTLE (YEP, THAT'S SOPHIE ON THE LABEL) OF COLOUR-CHANGING GIN, THIS IS A RELATIVELY NEW COCKTAIL BUT WE'VE NOW MADE IT A PERMANENT PART OF THE COCKTAIL BOARD.

SERVES 2

lots of ice
100ml (3½fl oz) good-quality gin (we use Pink Marmalade gin)
juice of ½ lemon or lime
100ml (3½fl oz) cranberry juice
1 teaspoon agave syrup (depending on the sweetness of your cranberry juice, you may need a little extra)
2 lavender sprigs, to serve (optional)

Fill a couple of martini glasses with ice and leave to chill.

Add plenty of ice to your cocktail shaker and throw in all your ingredients with panache! Pop the lid on the shaker and shake vigorously for 20 seconds – give it your all!

Throw out the ice from your now icy-cold glasses and pour your cocktail evenly into them. Top each with a lavender sprig, if you like, and drink immediately.

BRAMBLE

A SWEET AND COSY AUTUMNAL COCKTAIL. AND WHILE IT ISN'T
AS FLASHY AS SOME, IT STILL LOOKS GOOD IN YOUR GLASS.

SERVES 2

lots of ice, crushed and cubed
100ml (3½fl oz) good-quality gin
1 tablespoon maple syrup
juice of 1 lemon
1 tablespoon crème de mûre
    (or crème de cassis)

TO GARNISH
4 blackberries
2 rosemary sprigs

Fill 2 tumbler-style glasses with lots of crushed ice and set aside
to chill.

Fill your cocktail shaker with ice cubes, then add the gin, maple
syrup and lemon juice. Pop the lid on the shaker and shake
vigorously for 20 seconds, or until the shaker is too cold to handle.

Strain the cocktail through a fine sieve or cocktail strainer into the
ice-filled glasses. Drizzle the crème de mûre equally over the top of
the drinks, so you get a cool bleeding effect down through the ice.
Top each with a couple of blackberries and a little rosemary sprig
and serve.

COSMOPOLITAN

PACKS A BIT OF A PUNCH, AND HOLDING THE GLASS MAKES YOU
FEEL LIKE YOU'RE HAVING A BIG NIGHT OUT IN NYC.

SERVES 2

lots of ice
100ml (3½fl oz) good-quality
    vodka
50ml (2fl oz) Cointreau
50ml (2fl oz) cranberry juice
squeeze of orange juice
juice of ½ lime

TO GARNISH
2 pared strips of lemon or orange
    zest (use a vegetable peeler
    for this)

Fill your favourite cocktail glasses with ice and set aside.

Add plenty of ice to a cocktail shaker, then add the remaining
ingredients. Pop the lid on the shaker and shake vigorously for
about 30 seconds.

Throw out the ice from your now-chilled glasses and strain the
cosmo through a sieve or a cocktail strainer between each glass.
Twist the lemon or orange peel over and serve immediately.

POMEGRANATE NIGHTS

WELL DOESN'T THIS JUST SOUND EXOTIC! THE PERFECT DRINK FOR WHEN YOU WANT TO FEEL LIKE YOU'VE GONE AWAY SOMEWHERE HOT AND GLAMOROUS. THE POMEGRANATE IS SUCH AN UNDERRATED FLAVOUR AND BRINGS ITS SUBTLE SWEETNESS TO THE PARTY.

SERVES 2

100ml (3½fl oz) good-quality gin
40ml (scant 3 tablespoons) pineapple juice
4 teaspoons agave syrup
juice of 1 lime
plenty of ice
100ml (3½fl oz) pomegranate juice
a splash of sparkling water
a few pomegranate seeds, to garnish

Pour the gin, pineapple juice, agave syrup and lime juice into a cocktail shaker and half fill it with ice. Pop the lid on and shake vigorously for 30 seconds.

Fill 2 tall glasses with ice, then equally pour the pomegranate juice between each glass. Slowly strain the cocktail through a fine sieve or cocktail strainer into each glass. Top with a splash of sparkling water and a few pomegranate seeds and serve.

OLD FASHIONED

THIS ONE IS DON DRAPER IN A GLASS. GROWN UP AND WARMING, IT'S THE PERFECT NIGHTCAP.

SERVES 1

2 teaspoons golden caster sugar (or I like to use a brown sugar cube)
1–2 dashes of Angostura bitters
splash of water
ice
4 tablespoons Woodford Reserve bourbon whiskey

TO GARNISH
twist of orange peel
1 maraschino cherry (optional)

Put the sugar, bitters and water in a small tumbler-style glass and mix until the sugar dissolves. Alternatively, put a couple of dashes of bitter directly onto a sugar cube and crush it up in the bottom of the tumbler with a splash of water.

Fill the glass with ice, add the whiskey and stir for about 40 seconds. Garnish with a twist of orange peel and a cherry, if liked.

THE CHARMING BASTARD

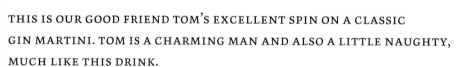

THIS IS OUR GOOD FRIEND TOM'S EXCELLENT SPIN ON A CLASSIC GIN MARTINI. TOM IS A CHARMING MAN AND ALSO A LITTLE NAUGHTY, MUCH LIKE THIS DRINK.

SERVES 1

50ml (2fl oz) gin
25ml (1fl oz) extra-dry vermouth
a splash of Amaro Montenegro (Italian liqueur)
ice
lemon twist, to serve

Stir all the ingredients in a cocktail shaker or pint glass half filled with ice for around 20 seconds, then strain through a cocktail strainer or fine sieve into a classic Martini glass. Garnish with a lemon twist, to serve.

TOMMY'S MARGARITA

YOU'RE NOT SUPPOSED TO HAVE A FAVOURITE CHILD, BUT A FAVOURITE COCKTAIL IS POSITIVELY ENCOURAGED! TOMMY'S IS IN AT THE NUMBER ONE SPOT FOR US BOTH. THE PERFECT PARTY STARTER AND ESSENTIAL FOR A MEXICAN FEAST. IT MAKES YOU A BETTER DANCER, TOO.

SERVES 2

ice
100ml (3½fl oz) tequila
50ml (2fl oz) lime juice
    (about 1 lime)
40ml (scant 3 tablespoons)
    agave syrup

TO SERVE
fine salt
lime half
ice

Stick 2 rocks glasses in the freezer for a bit for that frosty effect (I actually do this with all cocktail glasses before making cocktails).

Fill a cocktail shaker with ice and add all the cocktail ingredients. Pop the lid on and shake vigorously for 30 seconds.

When the glasses are really cold, pour some salt onto a small plate, run the lime half around the rim of each glass, then twist the glasses into the salt to coat the rims.

Fill each glass with ice and pour in the margarita to serve.

uncle Jackson's negroski

WE LOVE A NEGRONI ROUND HERE, BUT SOMETIMES NECESSITY IS THE MOTHER OF DRINKING A SIMILAR COCKTAIL WITH A SLIGHTLY DIFFERENT NAME. WHEN WE FOUND OURSELVES ON TOUR ONE SUMMER, TOASTING THE END OF A RUN OF HAPPY FESTIVAL DATES, WE REALISED WE WERE WITHOUT THE FULL COMPLEMENT OF NEGRONI INGREDIENTS. HOWEVER, UNCLE JACKSON (WHO PLAYS DRUMS IN THE BAND) SAVED THE DAY! WE HAD CAMPARI, WE HAD VERMOUTH, WE HAD VODKA, SO JACK MADE THESE DELICIOUS NEGROSKIS. AS THE RUSSIANS SAY, ZDA-RÓ-VYE! (TO YOUR HEALTH!)

ice
25ml (1fl oz) vodka (replace with
    gin for the classic recipe)
25ml (1fl oz) Campari
25ml (1fl oz) vermouth rosso

SERVES 1

Stir all the ingredients in a cocktail shaker or pint glass half filled with ice for around 20 seconds, then strain through a cocktail strainer or fine sieve into a classic rocks glass (or a paper cup filled with ice if you happen to be on a tour bus).

PICANTE MARGARITA PITCHER

YES PLEASE! MARGARITA IS OUR GO-TO PARTY FAVOURITE SO WHY NOT MAKE ENOUGH TO GO ROUND?

SERVES 6

plenty of ice
juice of 6 limes
300ml (10fl oz) Reposado tequila
150ml (5fl oz) Cointreau
1 fresh jalapeño pepper, sliced
3 coriander sprigs

TO GARNISH
2 tablespoons Tajin seasoning (if you can't find this in the supermarket, fine salt is great too)

Fill a large jug or pitcher with loads of ice. Squeeze the fresh lime juice into the pitcher, saving one of the lime halves unsqueezed.

Pour the Tajin seasoning (or salt, if using) onto a small plate. Rub the final lime half around the rims of your glasses, then dip the glasses into the seasoning until you have evenly coated them around the rims.

Add the remaining ingredients to the pitcher. Using a wooden spoon, stir the liquid in a clockwise motion for about 1 minute, or until it's all really cold.

Pour into your glasses and drink immediately.

You can also make the mixture ahead and simply add the ice at the last minute.

BLOODY MARY

ALWAYS A FAN OF A DRINK THAT'S ALSO A MEAL. THIS TOMATO JUICE CLASSIC DOESN'T HAVE TO BE JUST FOR THE MORNING AFTER AND IF YOU LIKE THE SPICY SIDE OF THINGS, DON'T BE AFRAID TO RAMP UP THE HEAT. SHE CAN TAKE IT!

plenty of ice
100ml (3½fl oz) good-quality vodka
500ml (18fl oz) tomato juice
zest and juice of ½ lemon
Worcestershire sauce
Tabasco sauce
good grating of fresh horseradish
pinch each of sea salt flakes and black pepper

TO GARNISH
2 leafy celery sticks

SERVES 2

Fill a jug with plenty of ice. Pour in the vodka and tomato juice, then add the lemon zest and juice. Add 6 shakes each of the Worcestershire and Tabasco sauces, grate in the horseradish and season to taste with the salt and pepper. Stir vigorously for about 40 seconds.

Pour the cocktail into tall glasses. Add a celery stick to each glass and serve.

WHITE LADY GIN SOUR

THIS REALLY REMINDS US OF OUR EARLY KITCHEN DISCOS AS WE HAD IT FOR THE FIRST TIME AFTER ONE OF THEM. IT'S AN UNEXPECTED DRINK REALLY... PART SMOOTH WITH THE EGG WHITE, PART PUNCHY WITH THE SOUR, BUT ALL ROUND WE LIKE IT.

SERVES 2

lots of ice
100ml (3½fl oz) good-quality gin
50ml (2fl oz) Cointreau
freshly squeezed juice of 1 lemon
4 teaspoons maple syrup
1 free-range egg white

Fill your favourite cocktail glasses with ice and set aside.

Add lots of ice to a cocktail shaker, then add all the remaining ingredients. Pop the lid on the shaker and shake vigorously for 40–50 seconds.

Strain through a sieve or cocktail strainer over the ice in your chilled cocktail glasses and drink immediately.

SHIRLEY TEMPLE FOR THE KIDS

IN OUR HOUSEHOLD THIS IS FOR THE KIDS BUT IT DOESN'T HAVE TO STOP THERE. THIS IS A VINTAGE CLASSIC TO MAKE SURE NO ONE HAS AN EXCUSE NOT TO GET INVOLVED. PLUS YOU GET CHERRIES! MAKE MINE A DOUBLE!

SERVES 2

plenty of ice
400ml (14fl oz) ginger ale
splash of grenadine
squeeze of lime juice

TO GARNISH
4 maraschino cherries

Fill up your favourite glasses for the kids with plenty of ice. Pour the ginger ale between the glasses, then add a splash of grenadine to each. Squeeze in a little lime juice and top each one with a a couple of cherries to serve.

GLOSSARY

UK	US
apple cider	hard apple cider
aubergine	eggplant
baking paper	parchment paper
beef burger	hamburger
beef shin	beef shank
bicarbonate of soda	baking soda
blitz	process in a food processor or blender
bombay mix	Indian spicy snack mix that includes rice sticks and fried lentils, peanuts, chickpeas, and onions
button mushrooms	white button mushrooms
caster sugar	superfine sugar
cavolo nero	tuscan kale or black-leaf kale
chicory	Belgian endive
chilli flakes	red pepper flakes
chips	fries; the sticklike shape of a fry
chopping board	cutting board
clingfilm	plastic wrap
coriander	fresh cilantro (unless ground and referring to the seed)
cornflour	cornstarch
courgette	zucchini
crème de mûre	a blackberry liqueur; can substitute with a black currant liqueur
demerara sugar	can substitute with raw brown sugar
double cream	heavy cream
egg, large	US extra-large egg
egg, medium	US large egg
electric whisk	electric mixer
farmhouse-style bread	country-style bread
fast-action dried yeast	active dry yeast
filo pastry	phyllo pastry
fish fingers	fish sticks
fish sauce	thai fish sauce
flaked almonds	slivered almonds
fridge	refrigerator
full-fat milk/cream/mayonnaise	whole milk/cream/mayonnaise
gas hob	gas stove
ghee	clarified butter
gherkin	pickle
griddle pan	ridged grill pan
grill	broiler, broiler pan
groundnut oil	peanut oil

UK	US
haricot beans	navy beans
icing sugar	confectioners' sugar
jacket potato	baked potato
jug	liquid measuring cup or pitcher
kitchen paper	paper towels
knob	small piece, such as pat of butter
maris piper potatoes	a type of floury potato; use Yukon Gold as a substitute
mince, beef/pork/lamb	ground beef/pork/lamb
mustard powder	dry mustard
natural yogurt	plain yogurt
nozzle (for a piping bag)	tip (for a pastry bag)
overleaf	following page
pepper (eg, red pepper)	bell pepper
palette knife	spatula
piping bag	pastry bag
plain flour	all-purpose flour
prawns	shrimp
rocket	arugula
rump steak	sirloin steak
runny honey	golden honey
salad leaves	salad greens
Savoy cabbage	use any green cabbage as a substitute
self-raising flour	use all-purpose flour plus 1 teaspoon baking powder per 4½oz of flour; UK self-raising flour does not include salt
shortcrust pastry	basic pie dough
sirloin steak	strip or tenderloin steak
skewer	such as one used for BBQ kabobs; can substitute with a toothpick
spatchcock	butterflied
sponge fingers	ladyfingers
spring onion	scallion
stock cube	bouillon cube
stone (eg an avocado)	pit (eg an avocado)
streaky bacon	normal bacon
strong bread flour	bread flour
tart case	tart shell
tea towel	dish towel
Tenderstem broccoli	Broccolini
tomato purée	tomato paste
tortilla, Spanish	Spanish potato omelet

index

acknowLeDGeMeNTs

We're thankful for all the nourishing good stuff – the food we eat and those who eat with us. Everything tastes better when we're with the right people: family who are friends and friends who are family.

Sonny, Kit, Ray, Jesse and Mickey – this book is for you from your Ma and Pa.

Thanks also to Octopus for making our cookbook dream come true.

First published in Great Britain in 2022 by Hamlyn, an imprint of
Octopus Publishing Group Ltd
Carmelite House
50 Victoria Embankment
London EC4Y 0DZ
www.octopusbooks.co.uk

An Hachette UK Company
www.hachette.co.uk

Distributed in the US by
Hachette Book Group
1290 Avenue of the Americas
4th and 5th Floors
New York, NY 10104

Distributed in Canada by
Canadian Manda Group
664 Annette St.
Toronto, Ontario, Canada M6S 2C8

ISBN (UK): 978 0 60063 729 5
ISBN (USA): 978 0 60063 747 9

A CIP catalogue record for this book is available from the
British Library.

Printed and bound in China

10 9 8 7 6 5 4 3 2 1

Food and cover photography by Issy Croker
Recipe development and food styling by Emily Ezekiel
Framed photography and illustrations used with kind
permission from Sophie Ellis-Bextor and Richard Jones.

Publishing Director: Eleanor Maxfield
Art Director: Yasia Williams
Senior Editor: Pauline Bache
Production Controller: Lisa Pinnell

Celsius oven temperatures are for a fan-assisted oven. If using a
conventional oven increase the temperature by 20°C/25°F/
½ Gas Mark.
Standard level spoon measurements are used in all recipes.
1 tablespoon = one 15 ml spoon
1 teaspoon = one 5 ml spoon
Both imperial and metric measurements have been given in all
recipes. Use one set of measurements only and not a mixture of both.
Eggs should be medium unless otherwise stated. The Department
of Health advises that eggs should not be consumed raw. This book
contains dishes made with raw or lightly cooked eggs. It is prudent
for more vulnerable people such as pregnant and nursing mothers,
the elderly, babies and young children to avoid uncooked or lightly
cooked dishes made with eggs. Once prepared these dishes should
be kept refrigerated and used promptly.
Milk should be full fat unless otherwise stated.
Fresh herbs should be used unless otherwise stated. If unavailable
use dried herbs as an alternative but halve the quantities stated.
This book includes dishes made with nuts and nut derivatives. It
is advisable for customers with known allergic reactions to nuts
and nut derivatives and those who may be potentially vulnerable
to these allergies, such as babies and children with a family history
of allergies, to avoid dishes made with nuts and nut oils. It is also
prudent to check the labels of pre-prepared ingredients for the
possible inclusion of nut derivatives.
Vegetarians should look for the 'V' symbol on a cheese to ensure
it is made with vegetarian rennet. There are vegetarian forms of
Parmesan, feta, Cheddar, Cheshire, Red Leicester, dolcelatte and
many goats' cheeses, among others.

Patterns on pages 32–3, 188–9, 204–5 and 208–9 used with kind
permission from Divine Savages, www.divinesavages.com
Patterns on pages 48–9, 78–9 and 124–25 used with kind permission
from Poodle & Blonde, www.poodleandblonde.com

Additional image credits: 13 *New Brighton* by Verney L Danvers for
British Railways, detail of poster, © National Railway Museum/
Science Museum Group Images, photo Antoine Pascal/akg-images;
39 *La Plage de Calvi*, Corse, by Roger Broders for PLM, detail of
poster © ADAGP, Paris and DACS, London 2022, photo Christie's
Images/Bridgeman Images; 67 *Tripoli, Libia* by G. Ferrari for FS,
detail of poster, photo AF Fotografie/Alamy Stock Photo; 85 *See
India* by Phanib Sanyal, detail of poster, photo CBW/Alamy Stock
Photo; 107 *Visit Japan by Japan Mail* by Yoshi for NYK Line, detail
of poster, photo Pictures from History/akg-images; 131 Dariia
Baranova/Dreamstime.com; 157, 201 illustrations by Alaver/
Shutterstock Creative; 179 *Why Bother About the Germans Invading
The Country? Invade it Yourself* by the Warbis Brothers for LPTB,
photo Shawshots/Alamy Stock Photo